# NOLO *Your Legal Companion*

*"In Nolo you can trust."* —THE NEW YORK TIMES

Whether you have a simple question or a complex problem, turn to us at:

## NOLO.COM

### Your all-in-one legal resource

Need quick information about wills, patents, adoptions, starting a business—or anything else that's affected by the law? **Nolo.com** features free articles in our Nolopedia, legal updates, resources and all of our books, software, forrms and online applications.

## NOLO NOW

### Make your legal documents online

Creating a legal document has never been easier or more cost-effective! Create an online will or trust, form an LLC, or file a Provisional Patent Application! Check it out at **http://nolonow.nolo.com**.

## NOLO'S LAWYER DIRECTORY

### Meet your new attorney

If you want advice from a qualified attorney, turn to Nolo's Lawyer Directory—the only directory that lets you see hundreds of in-depth attorney profiles so you can pick the one that's right for you. Find it at **http://lawyers.nolo.com**.

## ALWAYS UP TO DATE

### Sign up for NOLO'S LEGAL UPDATER

Old law is bad law. We'll email you when we publish an updated edition of this book—sign up for this free service at **nolo.com/ legalupdater**.

### Find the latest updates at NOLO.COM

Recognizing that the law can change, we post legal updates during the life of this edition at **nolo.com/updates**.

### Is this edition the newest? ASK US!

To make sure that this is the most recent edition available, just give us a call at **800-728-3555**.

(Please note that we cannot offer legal advice.)

## Please note

We believe accurate, plain-English legal information should help you solve many of your own legal problems. But this text is not a substitute for personalized advice from a knowledgeable lawyer. If you want the help of a trained professional—and we'll always point out situations in which we think that's a good idea— consult an attorney licensed to practice in your state.

1st edition

# Smart Policies for Workplace Technologies

## Email, Blogs, Cell Phones & More

By Attorney Lisa Guerin

| FIRST EDITION | JANUARY 2009 |
| Editor | RICHARD STIM |
| Cover Design | JALEH DOANE |
| CD-ROM Preparation | ELLEN BITTER |
| Proofreading | ROBERT WELLS |
| Index | MEDEA MINNICH |
| Printing | DELTA PRINTING SOLUTIONS, INC. |

Guerin, Lisa, 1964-
  Smart policies for workplace technologies : email, blogs, cell phones & more / by Lisa
Guerin. -- 1st ed.
     p. cm.
  ISBN-13: 978-1-4133-0926-3 (pbk.)
  ISBN-10: 1-4133-0926-7 (pbk.)
  1. Personal Internet use in the workplace. 2. Business enterprises--Computer networks-
-Security measures. 3. Telecommunications. 4. Blogs. I. 1. Title.
  HF5549.5.P39G84 2009
  651.7--dc22

                            2008031656

Quantity sales: For information on bulk purchases or corporate premium sales, please contact
the Special Sales Department. For academic sales or textbook adoptions, ask for Academic
Sales. Call 800-955-4775 or write to Nolo, 950 Parker Street, Berkeley, CA 94710.

## About the Author

Lisa Guerin is an editor at Nolo specializing in employment law. She is the author or co-author of several Nolo books, including *The Manager's Legal Handbook*, *Dealing With Problem Employees*, *The Essential Guide to Federal Employment Laws*, *The Essential Guide to Workplace Investigations*, *Create Your Own Employee Handbook*, *The Progressive Discipline Handbook*, and *Nolo's Guide to California Law*. Ms. Guerin has practiced employment law in government, public interest, and private practice, where she represented clients at all levels of state and federal courts and in agency proceedings. She is a graduate of Boalt Hall School of Law at the University of California at Berkeley.

# Table of Contents

# Appendixes

## B  Acknowledgment Form

# Index

# Drafting Effective Technology Policies

I n the not-so-distant past, every telephone had a cord tethering the caller to a nearby wall. The only way a business could transmit a document was to place it an envelope and pay someone to carry it to the recipient. To research important data, we had to find the right books, sometimes by traveling to a library, then take them off the shelf, open them, and hope that the table of contents would point us to the relevant pages.

For anyone under 20 years old, these must some seem like some outdated and inefficient limitations for operating a business. Nowadays, smartphones, email, the Internet, and other innovations have brought huge gains in business efficiency and productivity, allowing instant communication and access to information that would have seemed unimaginable only a short time ago.

And, of course, the technology wave hasn't crested yet. Every time we turn around, there's a new device—or an innovative way to use something we've already got—that could revolutionize the way we work. One day, not too long from now, we'll look back on iPhones, MySpace, and spam with the same nostalgia we reserve for the inkwell, carbon paper, and the IBM Selectric.

But no matter how technology evolves, one thing remains constant: New technology always brings new risks for employers. Technology can always be misused, either intentionally or accidentally. And, because employers are often legally responsible for the acts of their employees, technological developments have exponentially increased the possibility of legal exposure.

In recent years, we've been inundated with tales of employer woes: private customer information accidentally made public; racist or sexist jokes transmitted through a company's email system; employees causing car accidents while doing business on their cell phones; blogs that reveal company trade secrets; and widespread viewing of pornography at work. Although technology has promised to increase efficiency and rid us of documentation, it sometimes seems to have had the opposite effect—for example, companies now spend thousands of dollars combing through their electronic files to produce evidence for auditors, courts, and government agencies.

How does an employer modulate this digital din? Some try to control technology with other technology—for example, software that blocks certain Internet sites, programs that scan email for illegal content, or company-wide adoption of digital passwords to prevent access to company secrets. But fighting technology with technology is a never-ending game of cat and mouse, as the makers of anti-spam software have learned. There's always a way to skirt these technological solutions, which means companies have to develop a response to the workaround, and the escalation continues.

## Ten Ways Around Your Company's Technological Controls

Many companies, especially those with a savvy IT department, rely on blocking software, filters, and other technology to prevent employees from wasting resources or compromising security by, for example, surfing porn sites, sending large files, or storing work-related documents online. If the employees are also tech-savvy, however, they can get around these controls—and they often want to, because it's easier and more convenient. Often, these employees aren't troublemakers; they're just trying to work from home or save more email messages than your company's system allows.

This is one reason why your company must not only physically block employees from misusing company technology, but also adopt a policy prohibiting it and explaining why it's important. Employees who know the risks of getting around the company's controls are more likely to think twice before taking that shortcut. And if you're thinking your company's employees probably don't know the first thing about circumventing the company's controls, you better hope they don't read *The Wall Street Journal*, which published a list of ten controls and how to get around them. It explains how to:

- **Send large files:** Use an online service to send large files free.
- **Use software the company doesn't allow employees to download:** Access a Web-based version of the software or load it on a portable device.

## Ten Ways Around Your Company's Technological Controls (continued)

- **Visit blocked websites:** Use a proxy site to see the blocked website rather than visiting it directly, either through a search or by asking Google to do an English-to-English translation of the site (which calls it up on the searcher's screen).
- **Erase tracks from a company-issued laptop:** Use the browser to delete the history of websites visited.
- **Search for work documents from home:** Use software available from Google, Microsoft, or Yahoo! to store copies of files from one computer online, to be searched from another computer.
- **Store work documents online:** Use an online storage service or send files from work to a personal email account.
- **Evade company monitoring of Web-based email:** Encrypt messages or use a secure email session.
- **Access work email remotely:** Automatically forward all work-related email to a personal account.
- **Access personal email from a company-issued BlackBerry:** Add a personal email account to your profile at your BlackBerry's service provider website.
- **Avoid getting caught surfing the Web:** Hit Alt-Tab to minimize one window and maximize another.

Vauhini Vara, "Ten Things Your IT Department Won't Tell You," *The Wall Street Journal,* July 30, 2007.

A better approach is to adopt a set of commonsense rules that explain how employees should use the technologies the company makes available to them. Of course, policies alone won't stop all employee misconduct—there will always be employees who act badly, no matter what your company's handbook says. But policies, combined with training, leadership by example, and consistent enforcement, will help your company make sure that employees are using its electronic resources as the company intends.

And, if an employee doesn't follow the rules, policies provide a strong measure of legal protection if your company has to discipline or fire the employee, or prove that it did everything it could to prevent the incident (in the unfortunate event someone was harmed by an employee's misuse of technology).

This book provides policies you can adapt for your workplace on email use, employee blogs, using cell phones for work, downloading software, Internet access, and much more. It also provides the information you need to decide whether to use a particular policy and how to customize it to fit your workplace. The CD-ROM included with this book has all of the policies you'll need to make your workplace safe for technology.

---

### Chips and Scanners: What's Next for Workplace Tech

Most of the electronic tools covered in this book will be familiar to you. Even if you don't own a BlackBerry or use instant messaging, you're probably familiar with these commonplace innovations. On the horizon, however, are some truly sci-fi technology applications, some of which have already been adopted in the workplace.

A lot of these innovations are intended to be used on employees, not necessarily by them. Devices once used to track packages are now being used to track people. And, developments in biometrics are being pressed into service as employee identification devices. Here are some examples:

- **Global positioning devices.** GPS devices are used not only to keep tabs on pets, children, and valuable merchandise, but also to monitor the fleets—and employees—at FedEx and United Parcel Service (UPS).
- **Radio Frequency Identification (RFID).** RFID isn't just used to identify and track people and products via a tag or transponder; it's also being used to maintain business security and track

## Chips and Scanners: What's Next for Workplace Tech (continued)

employees' movements within a facility. (The RFIDs are commonly planted in employee ID badges.) At least one company has asked employees to have an RFID chip implanted in their arms to access the company's data center. These developments have led some states to pass laws prohibiting involuntary microchipping. (Nightclub owners have also discovered a use for RFIDs—to identify VIP customers and allow them to run a tab at the bar.)

- **Biometrics.** Verifying a person's identity through their unique physical characteristics is nothing new; police departments have been using fingerprints for this purpose for decades. But some companies are now pressing this technology into use to identify employees. At McDonalds, for example, employees clock in by scanning their hands rather than punching in a time card. Some companies use facial recognition and retina scanning systems to authenticate the identity of employees entering secured areas of a facility.

Use of these technologies on employees has met with a lot of resistance, and it's no wonder why: There's a disturbing level of intrusion involved in having a chip implanted in your body or having your every move tracked. Once this information is gathered, there's also the problem of keeping it safe. Identity theft is one thing, but what about the possibility of having your facial features "hacked" and misused, or having the government subpoena records of your movements, captured through a GPS or RFID system? The legal battles over these technologies are just getting started, so stay tuned.

# Why You Need Technology Policies

Your company probably has some written policies gathered in an employee handbook or policy manual, covering things like time off, benefits, employee conduct, and termination procedures. Unfortunately, however, many companies have neglected to keep up with the times by creating policies dealing with technology. Sometimes, the company's decision makers don't understand how technological innovations work or don't know how employees are actually using company resources. Sometimes, policy makers assume that existing policies are adequate to cover new technologies. Perhaps most often, however, the people responsible for writing policies just have too many other things to do, and put off updating their handbook to a later date.

---

CAUTION

**Practice makes policy.** A policy can exist without being written down or even communicated orally to employees. For example, if everyone in a company, from senior management on down, uses the company's email system for personal messages, that's company policy, even if the company has no official written guidelines saying that it's okay to use email in this way. The company would have a tough time defending a decision to fire an employee for sending personal messages if everyone else did so with impunity. It's a much better idea to consciously decide what your company's policies should be than to create policies by default.

---

If your company has procrastinated on drafting or updating its technology policies, you're missing an opportunity to protect the company's assets and leaving yourselves open to legal trouble in the future. Here are some ways that well-drafted technology policies can help your company.

## Protect Trade Secrets

Employees stealing trade secrets once had to stand over a copy machine, smuggle out boxes of documents, or bring in cameras. Today, however, the valuable intangible information upon which many companies are built—their trade secrets—can easily be purloined in digital format.

Technology policies can help protect against loss of company trade secrets, whether it occurs intentionally—as when an employee steals data to sell to a competitor or start a similar business—or unintentionally—as when an employee sends confidential inform- ation through Web-based email, which is hacked by an outsider. Even if your company faces an aggressive trade secret thief who doesn't care about the rules, strong policy language will help your company show that it took steps to protect its confidential information, which will work in your company's favor when it tries to stop others from using its stolen secrets.

## Preserve Customer and Employee Privacy

All companies keep some confidential information about their employees, whether Social Security numbers, next of kin, or medical records. Many companies also have confidential customer information, such as addresses, telephone numbers, and credit card accounts. Companies have a legal obligation (and obvious incentive) to maintain the privacy of this information, which up-to- date technology policies will help you do. Many states also require companies to notify consumers if their information is leaked, stolen, or otherwise compromised.

## Lessons From the Real World

**Technology policies help company prevent former employees from using its customer information.**

Andrew Verity and Christina Chang, a married couple, worked for Creative Marketing Concepts (CMC), a San Francisco company that sold merchandise branded with corporate logos. Verity left the company after efforts to negotiate a mutually agreeable severance arrangement fell through; Chang was fired shortly after for refusing to sign a nondisclosure agreement.

Here's why CMC might have wanted that agreement: After leaving CMC, Verity and Chang started their own business and allegedly solicited CMC's customers. CMC sued Verity and Chang for trade secret theft and asked the court to issue a restraining order prohibiting the couple from using its trade secrets or soliciting its customers. The couple filed a counterclaim, suing CMC for a number of alleged wrongs stemming from the termination of their employment.

At the heart of the lawsuit were CMC's alleged trade secrets: its client list and related information, such as purchasing history, sales volume, pricing, and buying habits. The court found that this information constituted a trade secret and ordered Verity and Chang not to use it in their business. The court also dismissed Chang's claim that she was wrongfully terminated for refusing to sign the nondisclosure agreement: Because CMC had legitimate trade secrets to protect, the court found that CMC could fire her because she wouldn't sign an agreement not to disclose them.

CMC's policies were an important piece of evidence in its favor. Under California law and the Uniform Trade Secret Act, a company must show that it took reasonable steps to maintain the confidentiality of its trade secrets. CMC met this requirement by showing, among other things, that its employee handbook included rules addressing trade secret theft, including prohibitions on taking home client files and forwarding company email without authorization.

*Lillge v. Verity,* 2008 Westlaw 906466 (N.D. Cal. April 1, 2008); *Lillge v. Verity,* 2007 Westlaw 2900568 (N.D. Cal. Oct. 2, 2007).

## 244 Million Breached Records ... and Counting

A stolen laptop here, a hacked website there, and the security breaches start to add up. According to the Privacy Rights Clearinghouse, more than 244 million records were compromised between January 2005 and the end of August 2008, and the number is increasing by the thousands daily. The Clearinghouse keeps an extensive database of security breaches involving consumer information (you can view it at www.privacyrights.org; select "A Chronology of Security Breaches" from the home page).

## Lay the Groundwork for Discipline and Termination

Policies provide the basis for employee discipline and termination by explaining what conduct is prohibited. Although most companies have the right to fire employees at will (that is, for any reason that's not illegal), it's always wise, for legal and practical reasons, to fire only for good cause. By putting employees on notice, technology policies make it more difficult for employees to later argue that they were treated unfairly or that they didn't know their conduct was prohibited.

CAUTION

**Policies must be enforced consistently.** Having policies on paper is a good first step, but it isn't enough to protect your company from wrongful termination lawsuits. To use a policy as a lawsuit defense strategy, your company must be able to show that everyone who violated the policy faced the same consequences. Otherwise, an employee can use your company's selective enforcement as proof of discrimination, retaliation, or other unfair treatment.

## Tell Employees That Their Communications Aren't Private

Because your company may one day have to read or monitor employee email and Internet browsing history, you should put employees on notice. It's only fair to tell employees ahead of time that their messages may be read. Notifying employees about monitoring will also deter them from sending inappropriate messages in the first place—your ultimate goal. What's more, employees' legal right to privacy is determined, in part, by how much privacy they reasonably expect to have. If your company tells employees their communications aren't private, it will be hard for them to argue later that they nonetheless expected confidentiality.

## Avoid Problems Caused by Employee Mistakes

Many of the problems created by workplace technology are the result of inadvertent errors—for example, clicking on an attachment that unleashes a virus—not intentional missteps. By setting ground rules for employees and explaining why those rules are important, technology policies can help your company avoid many of these problems in the first place.

## Conserve Company Resources

Misuse of technology—whether in the form of streaming audio, visiting illicit websites, or sending excessive personal email—costs time and money. Your company can preserve its bandwidth and server capacity, and maintain higher employee productivity, by adopting policies that limit how employees may use its technological resources.

## Limit Liability for Employee Misconduct

In some situations, your company can use its policies to show that it tried to prevent harm to others. For example, if your company has a

## Lessons From the Real World

**Company can read email, even if the employee has a confidential password.**

When Nissan hired Bonita Bourke to help employees with problems related to their computer system, the company probably had no idea just how much Ms. Bourke planned to use that computer.

The first sign of trouble was during a training session. In trying to demonstrate how dealership management could use email effectively, one of Ms. Bourke's coworkers pulled up a message at random to use as a teaching tool. Unfortunately for Ms. Bourke, it was a personal, sexual message that she had sent to another employee.

After the incident was reported to management, the company reviewed the entire workgroup's email messages. It found a number of personal messages, including messages with sexual overtones, sent by Ms. Bourke, who was fired.

Ms. Bourke sued Nissan for violating her privacy rights, among other things. The court ruled against her, however. Ms. Bourke had signed a form indicating her understanding that company policy restricted use of company computers to business purposes only. She also knew that email messages were occasionally read by someone other than the intended recipient. The court therefore found that, even though Ms. Bourke had a confidential password to use her computer, she could not reasonably expect her email messages to be private.

*Bourke v. Nissan Motor Corp.*, No B068705 (California Court of Appeal, 2nd District, 1993).

written policy prohibiting employees from making business-related calls while driving, that policy can be used as evidence that the company shouldn't be legally responsible for injuries an employee caused while doing just that.

## Manage Electronic Documents

Most of the innovations covered in this book allow employees to create, modify, and transmit documents electronically. They also create their own electronic records, in the form of logs, user records, browsing history, address books, and so on. Employers have a duty to preserve and hand over electronic documents like these in a lawsuit, just as if they were pieces of paper. Without policies telling employees how to manage their electronic documents, your company won't be able to meet these obligations. Lawsuits aside, if employees don't know which electronic documents to keep and where to put them, your company might not be able to access important records like contracts and customer orders.

# Creating Your Policies

This book will help you draft and update technology policies that will be effective in your company. What this book can't do, however, is tell you which policies are right for your company: That will depend on the industry, your corporate culture, the sophistication of your employees, your company's comfort level with risk, and plenty of other intangibles that will vary from company to company.

A large part of your job will be to decide how intrusive or trusting your company wants to be with its employees. This issue comes up again and again in the technology field because employee use of each of these devices and functions can be monitored. Here are some questions you may have to consider:

- Will your company read every employee email or will it simply reserve its right to monitor messages if it needs to?

- Will your company block access to certain Internet sites, monitor employee Internet traffic, or just tell employees not to visit certain types of sites?
- Will your company ban all camera phones at work or ask employees not to use them in certain areas?

## Employers' Duty to Retain and Hand Over Electronic Evidence

In December 2006, new rules took effect that define the obligations of lawsuit opponents to save and provide electronically stored evidence. The Federal Rules of Civil Procedure (FRCP), which apply to all noncriminal federal lawsuits, were updated to reflect that modern business documents are more likely to be stored on a server, disk, or backup tape than in a filing cabinet.

The FRCP now explicitly includes electronically stored information in the categories of documents and evidence that must be exchanged in discovery: the process of requesting and receiving information from the other side and from witnesses in a lawsuit. The rules have always obligated parties to discuss the case and exchange key evidence and witness lists early on (this is called the "meet and confer" requirement). Now, electronically stored information must be discussed and produced at this meeting, which is supposed to take place only a few months after a lawsuit is filed.

The rules impose a heavy obligation on companies to properly organize their electronic information so it can be accessed and reviewed quickly for a lawsuit. However, there's some good news here for companies that routinely purge emails and electronic information: There's no penalty if a party can't provide electronic data because it was lost as a result of the routine, good faith operation of an information system. But this "safe harbor" provision applies only until litigation is in the offing. Companies facing a lawsuit must immediately stop their purging, shredding, and deleting, and impose a "litigation hold." A company that destroys potentially relevant evidence after a lawsuit is imminent can face huge fines and penalties.

## Electronic Monitoring at Work

The American Management Association (AMA) has been surveying employers about their monitoring of employee activity since 2001. The most recent survey, for 2007, reveals that many employers monitor employee email and Internet activity. Here's what they're looking at:

- **Email.** 43% of the companies surveyed monitor employee email. Almost ¾ of those use technology to automatically review messages, and 40% have an actual human being read email. Perhaps as a result of this monitoring, 28% of the companies who responded to the survey had fired someone for misuse of email, mostly in the form of inappropriate or offensive language or violation of company rules.
- **Internet use.** Of the companies surveyed, ⅔ monitor employee Internet connections, and the same number block certain sites. 30% of the companies had fired someone for Internet misuse, with the vast majority of terminations resulting from viewing, downloading, or uploading inappropriate or offensive material.
- **Computer use.** 45% of the companies track content, keystrokes, and time spent at the keyboard, and almost the same number review computer files.
- **Outside sites.** 12% of responding companies monitor blogs to find out what's being said about them, and 10% monitor social networking sites.

You can find a summary of the survey's findings in the "Press Releases" area of the AMA's website, www.amanet.org.

Each chapter in this book covers a different type of electronic resource or function, such as email, camera phones, or blogs, providing an overview of the most important issues to consider, sample policy language, and information that will help your company decide whether—and how much—to regulate employee use of that equipment.

Although some policies should be adopted in every company (prohibiting employees from using cell phones while driving, for example), others are not so universal. That's why your first step in crafting technology policies is not to open this book to the appropriate chapter, but instead to figure out what your company is already doing and what it wants to do.

## Determine Your Current Practices

To get started, find out how technology is being used and regulated in your company now. First, consult your company's employee handbook or other written policies. Does your company have policies in place dealing with email, blogs, cell phones, and the other equipment addressed in this book? Are these policies up to date and adequate to address all of the technology your company and its employees currently use? Does your company require employees to sign acknowledgements of these policies?

Once you've collected and reviewed your company's written policies, it's time to get out of your office and talk to people to find out what's actually happening—what types of technology are actually in use, and in what ways. Here are some ideas to help you get started:

- **Talk to your IT department** (if your company has one). Find out what technologies your company supports and what it prohibits. Does IT have the capacity to read employee email and instant messages or to track employee Internet use? Is someone actually reading employee communications? Does the company block access to certain websites? Does the company provide cell phones, smartphones, or laptops to employees? Does it allow—or require—employees to use their own electronic devices for work? If so, are there any limits on the makes or models, or on an employee's ability to access the company's network? Is IT aware of any problems in employee use or misuse of equipment?

- **Interview company managers.** What technological resources do they use in their departments? Do they issue equipment to employees? Do they encourage employees to purchase their own equipment to use for work? Are they concerned about employee use of technology? Have they had to discipline or fire any employees for misusing electronic resources? What types of equipment do they need for their departments to function most efficiently and productively?

- **Consult with the lawyers.** Talk to your company's attorney to find out whether there are any special concerns—or past problems—you'll need to address. Has the company had to discipline or fire employees for electronic misconduct? Are there special concerns in your industry that you should consider? Do your state's laws or applicable court decisions address privacy and technology?

- **Get feedback from employees.** Find out what employees are really doing. Although you could talk directly to employees, you'll probably get more accurate results with an anonymous survey or questionnaire. Your goal is to find out how employees are really using the available technology, and in a face-to-face interview few employees will admit to things like sending personal email, visiting websites that aren't related to work, or getting around the company's electronic controls.

## Draft Policies

Don't be surprised or concerned if your interviews revealed confusion about your company's current policies and expectations, or differences in the way technology is used or managed in different departments. Your job now is to use that information to come up with policies that will work for the whole company and be enforced consistently in the future.

For each type of technology your company uses, go to the appropriate chapter in this book and review the policy language provided. Some chapters include alternatives to choose from, depending on how your company wants to handle a particular issue; some also include optional language you can include if, for example, you use monitoring software or provide employees with hands-free telephone equipment. Each chapter starts with a checklist of policy provisions, so you can make sure you've considered every important issue. Most readers should be able to put together effective policies using the language provided in the book and on the CD-ROM, with very few changes.

If, however, your company requires a different approach or wants to address additional concerns, you may need to draft or modify policy language. Here are a few rules to keep in mind:

- **Keep it simple.** Use short sentences and paragraphs, and easily understood vocabulary. Be as clear and concise as possible.
- **Know your audience.** Write in the language and style that reflects the culture of your company, and the education and sophistication of its employees.
- **Explain the policy.** When writing a technology policy, it's especially important to explain the purpose behind it. Employees who don't understand why it's important not to, for example, open an unscanned email attachment or send confidential information through Web-based email, might assume the company is just being paternalistic in imposing these requirements. Employees who know why a policy is necessary are more likely to follow it (and less likely to use workarounds).

## Review and Revise Policies

Once you've come up with draft policies, get some feedback. Ask the IT department and your company's managers to read them; they are the ones who are going to have to actually enforce the policies and field employee questions. They can let you know whether they think it will be difficult to implement a particular policy.

After you've considered this feedback and revised your policies, it's time to get a final review from a lawyer to be sure your technology policies are legally sound and up to date. A final legal review like this shouldn't take much time (or cost much money).

## Distribute Policies and Acknowledgment Forms

Now, it's time to pass out the policies. You should follow that with a meeting where you explain the policies and answer any questions employees might have. Tell employees that the company expects them to read the policies and abide by them, and ask employees to sign an acknowledgment form to that effect (you'll find an acknowledgment form in Appendix B and on the CD-ROM at the back of this book).

> CAUTION
> **Acknowledgment forms may be legally required.** Acknowledgment forms may look like overkill or a simple exercise in paperwork, but they are a vitally important part of your technology strategy. Currently, at least one state requires employers to get written consent from employees before monitoring their email and Internet use, and other states consider similar legislation every year. Even if they aren't legally required where your company does business, acknowledgment forms ensure that employees understand the rules for electronic communications, which will result in fewer violations of those rules and more protection for your company if it ever has to defend a decision to read employee communications.

It's a good idea to meet with employees to discuss any changes or additions to those policies. Use of technology is an area of major interest to employees, and one in which you may meet resistance. At a meeting, you can explain why the company needs these policies and what employees will have to do to comply.

## Enforce Policies

Your policies are only as good as the paper they're printed on unless your company puts them into action. Ignoring policy violations is a quick way to undo all of your work. Not only does it signal to employees that they don't have to follow the rules, but it also creates extra legal exposure. Adopting a policy shows that your company understands the risks of misusing a particular technology. If it ignores policy violations, your company is essentially saying, "We understand that this could create problems, but we've decided not to do anything about it."

For example, suppose company policy says employees will be issued hands-free equipment and must use it when driving and talking on a cell phone for business. The company hands out cell phones, but decides to put off purchasing headsets until the next fiscal year. An employee hits a pedestrian while taking a sales call. Here's what the pedestrian's lawyer might ask the human resources manager: "You wrote these policies, correct? And you said employees have to use hands-free technology because your company recognizes that's safer than allowing them to use handheld phones while driving, right? But your company never purchased hands-free devices, did it? And now, my client has been permanently injured because your company didn't want to spend $500, isn't that right?"

## Review Policies Annually and Update If Necessary

If you're in charge of keeping your company's employee handbook up to date, you probably don't read it from cover to cover when a review is required; you review only policies that may need to be changed because of a court ruling, new statute, or change in company practice. The truth is that most company policies aren't going to change from year to year.

In the technology arena, however, things change quickly and you may find these policies need periodic review. When you adopt a new policy or change the company's existing policy, meet with employees to explain what's new. As you did when you initially rolled out your tech policies, you should give employees time to read the policy, tell them why it was adopted, and answer any questions they might have. You should also prepare a new acknowledgment form.

Keep in mind, too, that this is just the beginning. Every year, there are new technology-related concerns on the horizon and your company's policies should address these issues as soon as they hit your radar screen.

## Considering New Technology?

After reading this book, you'll have a good idea of the kinds of issues you need to consider and address in your tech policies. You can use that expertise to help inform the company's decisions about new technology. Rather than just introducing a new gadget and waiting for the fallout, your company can plan ahead to avoid future problems. Here are some questions to brainstorm when your company is looking into new electronic resources:

- Why do we need this technology? Knowing how you want employees to use a particular device will help you make more informed decisions about purchasing, functionality, and appropriate limits for employees.
- Will we supply it for employees? If so, you'll have to think about how you will decide who gets one and whether you will limit personal use. If not, will you reimburse employees who purchase their own device? How will you limit security risks of employees linking to your network from, or keeping business information on, a personal device?
- Who will use this technology? If only the most senior management will be using a particular device, for example, your company may decide to forgo monitoring or extensive rules about personal use.
- What risks are associated with this technology? Are there new data security issues to consider? Safety concerns? A high risk of theft (as is true with many smaller devices) or abuse?
- What records does the device create? Because most technology creates a record, you'll need to consider whether your company should keep those records and in what form.
- Do we want to monitor employee use of the technology? If so, you'll need to make sure you have the resources and capability to handle it.

# Computers and Software

*In This Chapter:*

## Policy Provisions for Computers and Software

☐ Use of Computer Equipment

☐ Encryption and Encoding

☐ Software Use

Although many of us think of computers and the Internet as being joined at the hip, the computer—sans the Internet connection—remains a crucial business tool. Half of all U.S. employees work at computers, where they write documents, use spreadsheets, design graphics and artwork, put together presentations, track financial records, and more.

Because employees do the bulk of their work—and store it—on company computers, your company's policies must address several concerns. First, your company must be able to access its digital records and data if and when it needs to. Second, your company must protect its investments and make sure that computer equipment is not misused. Finally, your company must make sure that employees don't illegally use, copy, or download software programs.

---

### Which Software Is Most Often Pirated?

According to the Software & Information Industry Association, the five software titles most frequently pirated by companies in 2007 were:
- Symantec Norton Antivirus
- Adobe Acrobat
- Symantec PC Anywhere
- Adobe Photoshop
- Autodesk AutoCAD.

---

## Computers

Your computer use policy must address only a few basic issues; most of the details can be left to your other policies on specific computer activities such as email (discussed in Chapter 3), Internet access (discussed in Chapter 4), instant messaging (discussed in Chapter 5), and blogs and related issues (discussed in Chapter 6).

## Appropriate Use of the System

You should make sure employees know that their computers are company property, which the company may access at any time. In other words, the company has unfettered access to unfinished novels, vacation photos, spreadsheets of eBay sales, or any other private data that an employee saves to a company machine or hard drive. You should also require employees to limit their personal use of the computer system. The policy below spells out those limitations.

---

The Company may provide you with computer equipment and access to the Company's network in order to perform your job.

**Use of Computer Equipment**

The Company's computer equipment and network are intended for business use. You may use the Company's computer equipment for occasional personal purposes, but you may do so during nonwork hours only. Excessive personal use of the Company's computer equipment, even during nonwork hours, will be cause for discipline.

The Company has the ability to access and review all information stored on the Company's computer equipment and network. The Company reserves the right to perform such an inspection at any time, for any reason. You should not expect that any files, records, or other data stored on the Company's equipment and network will be private, even if you attempt to protect its privacy (for example, by using a password or designating it as "personal").

---

## Lessons From the Real World

**Employee's home computer can be searched.**

Robert Zieminski was an executive at TBG Insurance Services Corporation. TBG gave him two computers to use for work: One sat on his desk at the office, and the other was at his home.

Zieminski signed a company policy regarding use of its electronic and telephone equipment, which said in part that he would use the computers for business purposes only, that he would not use the equipment for "improper, derogatory, defamatory, obscene, or other inappropriate purposes," and that improper use of the computers could result in discipline, including termination. He also agreed that the company could monitor his computer use "as needed," and that his computer communications were not private.

The company fired Zieminski, claiming that he had repeatedly accessed pornographic sites on the Internet from his work computer. Zieminski filed a wrongful termination lawsuit, alleging that the company really fired him because a large portion of his stock in the company was about to vest; he also said that he never intentionally accessed porn sites, but instead that those sites simply "popped up" on his computer screen.

As part of the lawsuit, TBG asked Zieminski to hand over his home computer. Zieminski agreed to give back the computer, but insisted that he had to delete or destroy some personal information on the computer, which he contended was protected by his right to privacy. Zieminski claimed that, despite the monitoring policy he signed, employees understood that they could use their home computers for personal purposes, and that his computer included tax returns, personal correspondence, and records created by his wife and children. TBG countered that it had to see the computer intact in order to find out whether he accessed the same pornographic sites from home, which would tend to undermine his claim that those sites popped up on his work computer involuntarily.

The California Court of Appeals sided with TBG and required Zieminski to hand over the computer without deleting anything. TBG's policy put Zieminski on notice that his computer use could be monitored, and Zieminski signed that policy. Therefore, he could not argue that he had any reasonable expectation of privacy in the contents of his computer, even though it was in his home and was used by his family members.

*TBG Insurance Service Corp v. Superior Court of Los Angeles County,* 96 Cal.App.4th 4443 (Cal. App. 2nd District, 2002).

## Encryption and Encoding

Some of your company's employees may need to encrypt or encode sensitive information, especially if it is leaving the building virtually (on the Internet) or physically (on a computer disk or laptop). This is particularly true of employees who handle private customer or client data, medical records, and so on.

However, many employees have no business need to use encryption or encoding software. In that situation, the only real reason to use such software is to prevent their employer from reading their documents or email messages. It's wise to inform employees that encryption—except under the direction of the company—is prohibited. This policy reinforces the principle that employees should have no expectation of privacy in data on their computer (encrypted or otherwise); and that the company has the right to access all computer data all of the time. Further, prohibiting encryption lowers the possibility that company trade secrets, know-how, and data will disappear.

---

**Encryption and Encoding**

You may not encrypt or encode any files, data, or other information stored on the Company's computer equipment or network. If your job requires you to use encryption or encoding software, you may use it only for Company-related reasons and only with the permission of [_position authorized to allow encryption/encoding, such as "the IT director"_].

---

# Software

Some employees mistakenly believe that the company's $699 copy of Adobe InDesign is free for all to use, wherever and whenever they choose. In truth, the company does not own its copy of InDesign: It has paid $699 for a license to use it, usually only on one machine. If the license is violated—by employees or by the employer—the owner of the software can seek damages, often far exceeding the cost of the license, and the company will be on the hook.

Another big problem is software downloads from the Internet. Even if the download is legal (and many aren't; there are plenty of sites offering pirated software), it may well create a security risk for your company. Software downloads may include viruses and other malware that can infect your company's whole system. Typically, the employee isn't even aware of these risks because the download is disguised as a legitimate software program.

To avoid these problems, your software police should ban copying, installing, and downloading software without permission.

## Lessons From the Real World

**Company pays $500,000 to settle software piracy lawsuit.**

The Software & Information Industry Association (SIIA), a trade organization for the software and digital content industry, has been very active in pursuing those who pirate its members' products. It goes after not only those who sell illegal copies of software, but also those who use them—including companies that unwittingly violate their licensing agreements.

In January 2008, the SIIA settled a lawsuit against Whittiker Legal Publishing Corporation. The suit claimed that Whittiker had installed and used copies of software made by SIIA member companies (including Adobe, Filemaker, and Symantec) without the proper licenses. Whittiker agreed to pay half a million dollars, destroy the unlicensed software, purchase replacement software, and adopt comprehensive software management policies. Even though the company used a third-party vendor to manage its software needs, Whittiker bore the ultimate legal responsibility for compliance.

Although it isn't clear how SIIA learned of Whittiker's license violations, many of its enforcement actions stem from whistleblowers. The SIAA has an antipiracy program that encourages people to report corporate misuse of software, offering rewards to those whose tips pan out. In 2007, the SIAA received 427 tips, and paid out $52,000 in reward money. You can learn more at the SIIA's website, www.siia.net (under the "Programs" tab, select "Anti-Piracy").

**Software Use**

It is our Company's policy to use licensed software only in accordance with the terms of its license agreement. Violating a license agreement is not only unethical; it is also illegal and can subject the Company to criminal prosecution and substantial monetary penalties.

To help us adhere to this policy, employees may not do any of the following without permission from [*position authorized to approve software use, such as "the IT director"*]:

Copy any Company software program for any reason.

Install a Company software program on any computer (including your home computer).

Install a software program (including software licensed or owned by the employee) on any Company computer.

Download any software program from the Internet to a Company computer.

The Company may audit Company-owned computers at any time to ensure compliance with this policy.

CAUTION

**Don't forget the acknowledgment form.** If your company adopts the computer and software policy covered in this chapter, make sure you require employees to sign an acknowledgment form. You'll find a sample acknowledgment form and instructions in Appendix B; a blank acknowledgment form is included on the CD-ROM at the back of this book.

## Putting It All Together: Sample Computer and Software Use Policy

Here's a sample policy for computer and software use adopted by a publishing company. Employees use their computers and software all the time, and the company wants to make sure that it doesn't violate its software licensing agreements.

# Computer and Software Use Policy

The Company may provide you with computer equipment and access to the Company's network in order to perform your job.

## Use of Computer Equipment

The Company's computer equipment and network are intended for business use. You may use the Company's computer equipment for occasional personal purposes, but you may do so during nonwork hours only. Excessive personal use of the Company's computer equipment, even during nonwork hours, will be cause for discipline.

The Company has the ability to access and review all information stored on the Company's computer equipment and network. The Company reserves the right to perform such an inspection at any time, for any reason. You should not expect that any files, records, or other data stored on the Company's equipment and network will be private, even if you attempt to protect its privacy (for example, by using a password or designating it as "personal").

## Encryption and Encoding

You may not encrypt or encode any files, data, or other information stored on the Company's computer equipment or network. If your job requires you to use encryption or encoding software, you may use it only for Company-related reasons and only with the permission of the IT director.

## Software Use

It is our Company's policy to use licensed software only in accordance with the terms of its license agreement. Violating a license agreement is not only unethical; it is also illegal and can subject the Company to criminal prosecution and substantial monetary penalties.

To help us adhere to this policy, employees may not do any of the following without permission from the IT director:

Copy any Company software program for any reason.

Install a Company software program on any computer (including your home computer).

Install a software program (including software licensed or owned by the employee) on any Company computer.

Download any software program from the Internet to a Company computer.

The Company may audit Company-owned computers at any time to ensure compliance with this policy.

# Email

## In This Chapter:

### Policy Provisions for Email

☐ Use of the Email System

☐ Email Is Not Private

    ☐ Optional Policy Language for Monitoring That Flags Keywords

    ☐ Optional Policy Language for Random Monitoring

    ☐ Optional Policy Language for Keylogger Monitoring

☐ All Conduct Rules Apply to Email

☐ No Solicitation by Email

☐ Professional Tone and Content

☐ Guidelines for Email Writing

☐ Email Security

☐ Retaining and Deleting Email Messages

Perhaps more than any innovation covered in this book, email has revolutionized the way we work. Email can be terrifically efficient. It allows us to communicate quickly, send each other documents, work offsite, work in teams that are geographically dispersed, and document negotiations and decisions, all at warp speed.

But email also has its dark side. Every email message creates an electronic record—in effect, a document that a company might have to hand over in a lawsuit. In addition, the apparent informality of email encourages behavior that people might not engage in face to face, like "flaming," circulating inappropriate jokes, or sharing confidential information. And the speed and virtuality of email also make it easier to commit all manner of workplace misconduct, from harassment to trade secret theft.

## Email Bankruptcy

The typical information worker who uses a computer all day turns to his or her email program more than 50 times every day. Why? Because we are all inundated with email messages—more than 200 billion are sent every day, worldwide, according to recent news reports.

It's gotten so bad that even the companies that sell email services and products to the rest of us recognize the problem. Recently, Microsoft, Intel, and other technology firms joined together to study the issue of digital overload and come up with ways to manage our increasingly overflowing inboxes. One method they probably won't recommend is email bankruptcy: when a user facing an overwhelming pile of messages decides to get a "fresh start" be deleting all of them and starting over.

If you're having trouble believing that email can cause this much trouble, consider these statistics:

- Almost half of employees have sent or received emails that include jokes, stories, or pictures of a "questionable" nature (that is, with racy or sexual content, or that are politically incorrect). (2005 Harris Interactive Poll for Fortiva summary of findings available in the archived press releases at www.fortiva.com.)
- Six percent of employees have emailed confidential company information to someone they shouldn't have. (Gregg Keizer, "Email Spills Corporate Secrets," *InformationWeek*, December 12, 2005.)
- Although 92% of employees surveyed said that they had never sent an email that put their company at risk, 68% in fact had. (2005 Harris Interactive Poll for Fortiva.)
- More than a quarter of companies in a recent survey have fired an employee for email misuse; most of those terminations were for inappropriate or offensive language and violation of company rules. (2007 Electronic Monitoring & Surveillance Survey, conducted by the American Management Association and The ePolicy Institute; summary of findings available in the press release section of www.amanet.org.)
- Fifteen percent of companies have faced a lawsuit triggered by employee email, and almost one quarter of companies have had their email subpoenaed by courts and regulators. (2006 Electronic Monitoring & Surveillance Survey, conducted by the American Management Association and The ePolicy Institute; summary of findings available in the press release section of www.amanet.org.)

To reap the considerable benefits of email while keeping risks to a minimum, your company must adopt a sensible and comprehensive email policy and require employees to sign off on it. This chapter explains everything you'll need to cover, including personal use of email, email monitoring, archiving and retention of messages, rules on appropriate content, and more.

CROSS REFERENCE

**Information on personal Web-based accounts.** This chapter covers only the company's own email system. However, some employees use their company's Internet connection (or use handheld devices such as BlackBerries, iPhones, and Treos) to send and receive email on their own personal accounts (for example, Hotmail or Yahoo!). You can find more information on this issue in Chapter 4.

# Personal Use of Email System

The first decision to make is whether your company will allow employees to send personal email messages—messages to friends and family members, for example, or messages to coworkers about nonwork topics, such as sports, politics, or parties—using the company's equipment. Although some companies ban all personal use of their email systems, the better approach is to allow some personal use with restrictions.

## What Would You Give Up to Keep Your Email Access?

Many of us use email every day, some of us for hours a day. But how important is email to us? Would we be willing to give up other things we hold dear just to maintain our email access? According to a recent survey, the answer is a resounding "Yes!" Almost 75% of the respondents indicated that email is essential to their lives. So essential that they would be willing to forgo the following to keep it:

- More than half said they would give up chocolate.
- Half said they would give up coffee.
- More than 40% would give up television.
- Almost 40% would give up their cell phones.
- Almost 15% would give up their spouse or significant other.
- 6% would give up their home.

Sharon Gaudin, "Would You Give Up Deodorant or a Spouse for Email?" *InformationWeek*, April 17, 2007.

## Prohibiting All Personal Use

Some companies don't want employees to use their email systems for personal messages, period. After all, the equipment belongs to the company, personal messages take employees away from their work and create potential liabilities, and then there's the storage and bandwidth problem. So why not just ban all personal use?

For a simple reason: Everyone will break the rule. Some might not have an Internet connection at home; others might have a message that has to be sent immediately (like "I'll be home late" or "Can you pick up the kids' carpool today"). The truth is that a policy forbidding any personal use of email will probably be violated regularly by everyone from the CEO on down.

Because these policies are so often violated, they are seldom enforced, at least not consistently. Companies rarely have the time and energy to spend monitoring every transmission, then imposing discipline on everyone who sends a personal message. Instead, companies enforce the policy when an employee crosses the line by spending significant time on personal messages, sending large attachments, sending messages that include racial jokes or sexual material, sending out solicitations for a child's fundraising activities or a personal business, and so on. It's much easier—and safer, from a legal standpoint—to ban these types of misconduct rather than any and all personal use.

Any time an employer enforces a policy inconsistently, it takes a legal risk. An employee who is disciplined for violating the policy when others are not could point to that inconsistency as evidence of an illegal motive, such as discrimination or retaliation.

> EXAMPLE: Carla complains that her manager, Jim, has been sending her sexually explicit jokes on the company's email system. The company has a policy that prohibits all personal email, but it doesn't monitor employee email and has yet to enforce the policy.

The company begins its investigation by reviewing Carla's and Jim's email accounts. The investigator discovers Jim's harassing messages, but also discovers that Carla occasionally uses the company's email system for family matters, including corresponding with her children's teachers and coaches. The company gives Jim a written warning for misconduct; Carla receives a written warning for violating the company's email policy. Because Carla already has a written warning for performance problems, she is now ineligible for raises and promotions for a year.

Several weeks later, the company receives a demand letter from Carla's attorney. The claim? That Carla was retaliated against for complaining of sexual harassment. The letter states that other employees routinely used the email system for personal matters, but Carla was the only one disciplined—and only after she complained of possible sexual harassment. The company's attorney advises it to rescind Carla's written warning immediately and perhaps even consider a small monetary settlement. Even though Carla violated the policy, it looks too much like retaliation to enforce it for the first time against someone who had just raised concerns about harassment.

Inconsistent enforcement based on the content of the message could lead to legal problems as well. For example, if your company bans all personal messages but typically looks the other way when employees send them, it could face a discrimination claim if it disciplines an employee for sending out a message proselytizing for his or her religion or publicizing an upcoming event that has a particular ethnic or racial focus, such as a Cinco de Mayo parade or a conference for African American entrepreneurs.

Your company could even face an unfair labor practices charge if it disciplines only for messages relating to a union or other employee organizations, or to working conditions generally. The National Labor Relations Board, the federal agency that enforces the laws relating to unions and employee organizing, has consistently held that employers who single out these types of messages for discipline while allowing similar messages (for example, allowing messages about other organizations or meetings) could be violating the National Labor Relations Act.

For all of these reasons, policies that ban all personal use are impractical and invite legal exposure.

## Allowing Some Personal Use

To balance the company's interest in preventing a lot of personal use of its equipment against employees' desire to send occasional personal messages, consider policy language that allows some personal use. The policy provision below allows employees to send personal messages, but only outside of work hours and only at the company's discretion. It also leaves the company room to discipline an employee who taxes the system by sending files with gigantic attachments, spending hours conversing with friends, or sending "chain letter" correspondence to dozens of recipients.

You can (and should) further limit the types of messages employees may send and put them on notice that using email for harassment, for solicitation, or to transmit confidential information will lead to discipline; see "Content Rules," below.

---

**Use of the Email System**

The email system is intended for official Company business. Although you may use the email system occasionally for personal messages, you may do so during nonworking hours only. If you send personal messages through the Company's email system, you must exercise discretion as to the number and type of messages you send. You must also ensure that your personal use of the email system does not interfere in any way with your job duties or performance. Any employee who abuses this privilege may be subject to discipline.

---

# Privacy

Your email policy absolutely must inform employees that their messages are not private and must reserve the company's right to monitor and read messages at any time. Even if your company has no plans to actively monitor employee email, it may one day have to do so if an employee is accused of sending sexually harassing messages, transmitting trade secrets to a competitor, or using email to spread false rumors about another employee, for example.

You might be wondering why your company has to tell employees that it might read email messages that are sent on company equipment, especially if those messages might get the company in legal trouble. The answer lies in the way privacy law works. As applied to workplace issues, privacy law generally balances an employee's reasonable expectations of privacy against the employer's reasons for monitoring, searching, and so on. The more a company can do to diminish employee expectations of privacy, the more legal protection it has when monitoring employee communications. And one of the best ways to do this is by explicitly stating, in a written policy, that email messages are not private.

## Perceptions of Employers vs. Employees on Email Privacy

Many employees don't believe that employers have the right to read their email messages, even though virtually every court to consider the issue has found otherwise. According to a 2005 study by the Society for Human Resource Management (SHRM) and careerjournal.com, almost half of the employees surveyed did not agree that employers had the right to read employee email. In the same year, a survey conducted by the American Management Association showed that 55% of companies actually do monitor and review employee email.

## Lessons From the Real World

**Is an employee's email to an attorney confidential?**

One of the bedrock principles of the law is the attorney-client privilege, which protects the confidentiality of conversations between a lawyer and his or her client. In the past, employers had very few ways to get their hands on communications between an employee and a lawyer, which were likely to occur in person or by letter or personal phone call.

Today, however, there are some (admittedly risk-taking) employees who use company email to correspond with a lawyer—about suing the employer whose email system they're using. If the employer recovers those email messages, whether in the normal course of monitoring or as part of preparing to defend a lawsuit the employee later files, can it read them?

Courts have ruled different ways on this issue, depending largely on the company's policies and practices regarding email privacy. For example, one New York court found that a doctor who sent email messages to his lawyer on his employer's email system had waived the attorney-client privilege, because the employer's policy prohibited personal use of the system and notified employees that it monitored employee email. On the other hand, a federal court in the same state found that an employee had not waived the privilege by using a company-issued laptop to send email to her attorney from home, using her own AOL email account. Although the employer had a policy prohibiting personal use of its computers, that policy was not actively enforced. And, because the employee used her own email account, the messages were not stored on the employer's server.

*Scott v. Beth Israel Medical Center*, 847 N.Y.S. 3d 436 (N.Y. Sup. 2007); *Curto v. Medical World Communications, Inc.*, 2006 WL 1318387 (E.D. N.Y. 2006).

> **Email Is Not Private**
>
> Email messages, including attachments, sent and received on Company equipment are the property of the Company. We reserve the right to access, monitor, read, and/or copy email messages at any time, for any reason. You should not expect privacy for any email you send using Company equipment, including messages that you consider to be personal, or label with a designation such as "Personal" or "Private."

# Monitoring

If your company has monitoring software it plans to use, or if someone will be assigned to read employee email on a regular basis, you should let employees know in your written policy. After all, the purpose of an email policy is not only to allow the company to read those problematic messages after they've been sent, but also to deter employees from sending them in the first place. Telling employees that their messages will be monitored and/or read will almost certainly help accomplish this second goal.

**CAUTION**

**Choose your monitors wisely.** Before your company gives anyone unfettered access to their coworkers' email, it should consider this: According to a 2007 survey, one-third of IT administrators admit snooping through employee email, files, and other confidential information. (Manek Dubash, "Study: IT Admins Read Private Email," *PC World*, May 29, 2007.) These employees apparently had very little "need to know," but the opportunity to spy on their coworkers was just too tempting. If you choose to monitor, select your readers with great care—and check up to make sure that they aren't overstepping their authority.

Whether your company should regularly monitor employee email is a tough issue to sort through. Doing so will force employees to take the email policy seriously and thereby make them less likely to send messages that are harassing, threatening, or otherwise in violation of your policy. It's just human nature: We aren't as quick to break the rules if we think we will get caught.

But there are some serious downsides as well, with employee dissatisfaction topping the list. Employees don't want to feel like the company doesn't trust them or plans to check up on their every keystroke. Monitoring also costs time and money. And some employers just find monitoring distasteful. They don't want to be cast in the role of Big Brother.

Ultimately, the company's philosophy, workforce, and needs will determine whether the benefits of monitoring outweigh the disadvantages. If your company has no immediate plans to monitor or read employee email, you need not add additional monitoring language: The provision on privacy, above, is sufficient.

If, however, your company plans to regularly monitor messages, you should add that information to your policy immediately following the privacy provision, above. What your policy should say depends on how your monitoring software works. Here are some sample provisions:

---

**Optional Policy Language for Monitoring That Flags Keywords**

In addition, the Company's software automatically searches the messages you send for questionable content, including sexual or racial comments, threats, trade secrets, competitive information, and inappropriate language. Any message deemed questionable will be forwarded to, and read by, Company management.

**Optional Policy Language for Random Monitoring**

In addition, the Company will select and read employee messages at random to ensure that employees are in compliance with this policy.

**Optional Policy Language for "Keylogger" Monitoring**

In addition, the Company's monitoring software automatically creates a copy of every message you draft, even if you never send it. Company personnel will regularly read these copies to make sure that no employee violates this policy.

# Content Rules

Your policy should tell employees what types of messages are allowed and prohibited. It's also a good idea to remind employees what email is: an electronic record of a communication, which can be saved, printed, forwarded to unknown recipients, and otherwise leave the building.

## Harassment, Threats, and Other Misconduct

One of the most common email problems employers face is electronic harassment: sexually explicit content, lewd or racist jokes, inappropriate stories or name calling via the company's email system. Your policy should make clear that all other company policies relating to harassment and other misconduct apply equally to email.

**All Conduct Rules Apply to Email**

All of our policies and rules of conduct apply to employee use of the email system. This means, for example, that you may not use the email system to send harassing or discriminatory messages, including messages with explicit sexual content or pornographic images; to send threatening messages; or to reveal Company trade secrets or confidential information.

## Lessons From the Real World

**Employer has a duty to stop online harassment.**

Tammy Blakey was a pilot for Continental Airlines. In 1991, she began complaining that her male coworkers were leaving pornographic pictures in her cockpit and other work areas, and were making vulgar, gender-based remarks to her. Eventually, she filed a lawsuit against Continental for failing to stop this harassment.

While the lawsuit was proceeding, a group of male pilots began posting derogatory remarks about Blakey on an online computer bulletin board for Continental employees. Blakey sought to amend her complaint to add these comments as additional examples of harassment and defamation.

The New Jersey Supreme Court found that Blakey could sue based on the electronic bulletin board comments. Although an employer doesn't have a duty to monitor its employees, the court found, it does have a duty to stop harassment it already knows about—including harassment that takes place online.

*Blakey v. Continental Airlines*, 751 S.2d 538 (N.J. 2000).

## Solicitation

Many companies prohibit employees from soliciting other employees—for example, to buy products, support a particular political candidate, donate to a charity, or join a religious group. If your company has a no-solicitation rule, you should extend it to use of the email system.

In fact, even if your company doesn't prohibit solicitation, there's a recent legal decision that might make you reconsider. The National Labor Relations Board (NLRB) held that a company could use its general ban on email solicitation to discipline an employee who sent union-related messages. Although it would be discriminatory to single out union messages for discipline while allowing employees to send messages relating to other organizations, the NLRB found that a larger prohibition on all solicitation for outside groups was legal.

The policy language below prohibits the most common types of solicitation. You'll notice that the last sentence allows employees to ask permission to solicit donations to particular charities. This language allows your company to permit certain appeals (for example, to donate to the United Way or to purchase Girl Scout Cookies). If your company wants to ban all charitable appeals without exception, you can delete that part of the sentence.

---

**No Solicitation by Email**

You may not use the email system to solicit others to patronize an outside business or to support an outside organization, a political candidate or cause, or a religious cause. You also may not use the email system to ask employees to donate to a particular charitable cause without the prior consent of _____.

---

## Professional Tone and Content

Your policy should also remind employees that their email messages should be professional and appropriate.

---

**Professional Tone and Content**

We expect you to exercise discretion in using electronic communications equipment. When you send email using the Company's equipment, you are representing the Company. Make sure that your messages are professional and appropriate, in tone and content. Remember, although email may seem like a private conversation, email can be printed, saved, and forwarded to unintended recipients. You should not send any email that you wouldn't want your boss, your mother, or our Company's competitors to read.

---

## Netiquette

Your company may want to include some writing guidelines in its policy, especially if it has a lot of entry-level or otherwise inexperienced employees. Because email is seen as informal, some employees send out even work-related messages sprinkled with smiley-face icons and exclamation points, written in all lowercase or capital letters, or filled with acronyms or usages peculiar to the online world. Some employees also make the mistake of sending out email without considering its content or style, only later to regret having expressed anger too hastily or sending a message that doesn't look professional.

You can include as much or as little detail as you like about writing style. Here is a policy provision that includes a handful of common "netiquette" rules:

**Guidelines for Email Writing**

1. Always spell-check or proofread your email messages. Email is official Company correspondence. Spelling errors in email are all too common, and they look sloppy and unprofessional.

2. Use lowercase and capital letters in the same way that you would in a letter. Using all capital letters is the email equivalent of shouting at someone—and it can be hard on the eyes. Failing to use capital letters at all (to begin a sentence or formal noun) can confuse readers and seem overly cute. Unless you are writing poetry, use standard capitalization.

3. Remember your audience. Although email encourages informal communication, that might not be the most appropriate style to use if you are addressing the CEO of an important customer. And, remember that your email can be forwarded to unintended recipients, some of whom may not appreciate joking comments or informalities.

4. Don't use email for confidential matters. Again, remember the unintended recipient. Your email might be forwarded to someone you didn't anticipate or might be sitting at a printer for all to see. If you need to have a confidential discussion, do it in person or over the phone.

5. Send messages sparingly. There is rarely a need to copy everyone in the Company on an email. Carefully consider who really needs to see the message, and address it accordingly.

6. Always think before you send. Resist the urge to respond in anger, to "flame" your recipient, or to get emotional. Although email gives you the opportunity to respond immediately, you don't have to take it.

7. Don't leave the subject line blank. Always include a brief description, so readers will know what your email is about at a glance. This makes it easier for all of us to manage our email—and makes it more likely that you will receive a response to your message.

8. Don't overuse the "urgent" tag. Mark a message as urgent only if it is truly important and must be answered right away.

### Whoops!

Have you ever misaddressed an email, sent an email without a promised attachment, or gotten an email that you considered inappropriate? Well, you're not alone. According to a 2007 InformationWeek survey of more than 700 employees:

- 15 % said they'd received an email sent in anger.
- 13% said they'd gotten flirtatious email.
- 23% said they'd received email they considered politically incorrect.
- 20% had sent an email to the wrong person.
- Almost 40% had forgotten to include an attachment in an email they sent.
- A very sad 5% had received a humiliating message that was copied to others.

Anyone can make these mistakes or errors in judgment. Even those who really should know better, like, say, Microsoft, which accidentally sent a reporter an email message with a surprising attachment: an internal dossier its PR firm had compiled on the reporter. The reporter was writing a story on Microsoft's blogging initiative as evidence of the company's effort to be more transparent with the public. Ouch! You can read about in the Epicenter blog at *Wired*'s website, www.wired.com; the story appears in March 2007.

## Viruses and Other Security Threats

Your policy should give employees a few tips to help them avoid launching a virus, Trojan horse, worm, or other electronic threat on your company's email system.

**Email Security**

To avoid email viruses and other threats, employees should not open email attachments from people and businesses they don't recognize, particularly if the email appears to have been forwarded multiple times or has a nonexistent or peculiar subject heading. Even if you know the sender, do not open an email attachment that has a strange name or is not referenced in the body of the email—it may have been transmitted automatically, without the sender's knowledge.

If you believe your computer has been infected by a virus, worm, or other security threat to the Company's system, you must inform the IT department immediately.

Employees also may not share their email passwords with anyone, including coworkers or family members. Revealing passwords to the Company's email system could allow an outsider to access the Company's network.

## Retention and Deletion

Email messages create electronic records. Your email policy must tell employees how to manage those records—that is, which records to keep and which to delete.

Email messages often include important company records that it either should or is legally required to retain. For example, if applicants apply for a job by email, those email messages are hiring records that, like other hiring records, must be kept for three years. Of course, your company will also want to retain electronic contracts, agreements, records of negotiations, consent forms, and so on.

On the other hand, the great majority of email messages sent and received by your company's employees can—and should—be deleted as soon as they are dealt with. Email messages take up a lot of virtual space, and employees who are email packrats can quickly overload your company's storage capacity.

What's more, your company can be required to produce email messages if it is sued, just like it has to hand over paper documents. The more messages your employees keep, the more messages your company will have to comb through—and possibly hand over—if it is faced with a lawsuit. The Federal Rules of Civil Procedure (FRCP), which set the ground rules for federal lawsuits, were recently amended to require parties to a lawsuit to hand over electronic evidence just like any other evidence, not only when the other party asks for it in discovery but also as part of their pretrial disclosures.

However, the FRCP also acknowledge that electronic evidence is different from regular paper documents, in that it may be difficult to access because it's been destroyed in the regular course of business. Many companies have a practice of deleting email messages and writing over backup tapes after a certain period of time. A company won't face sanctions or penalties for failing to hand over electronic evidence if that evidence was destroyed because of the routine, good-faith operation of an electronic information system. If, for example, your company's email program automatically purges email messages after a certain number of days and reuses its storage capacity by writing over older information, it won't face legal trouble if it can't hand over messages that were destroyed in the regular course of business.

This protection doesn't extend to evidence that's destroyed after the company knows that it is (or might soon be) facing a lawsuit, however. Once this happens, the company has a legal duty to preserve all evidence that might be relevant to the case, including email messages and other electronic information. (This is commonly referred to as a "litigation hold.") If your company faces litigation, it will have to immediately override its usual purge procedures and make sure it hangs on to every applicable document.

**Retaining and Deleting Email Messages**

Because email messages are electronic records, certain messages must be retained for compliance purposes. Please refer to our record-keeping policy for guidance on which records must be kept, and for how long. If you have any questions about whether and how to retain a particular email message, please ask your manager.

Because of the large volume of emails our Company sends and receives each day, we discourage employees from storing large numbers of email messages that are not subject to the retention rules explained above. Please make a regular practice of deleting email messages once you have read and/or responded to them. If you need to save a particular message, you may print out a paper copy, archive the email, or save it on your hard drive or disk. The Company will purge email messages that have not been archived after _____ days.

The Company may have occasion to suspend our usual rules about deleting email messages (for example, if the Company's is involved in a lawsuit requiring it to preserve evidence). If this happens, employees will be notified of the procedures to follow to save email messages. Failing to comply with such a notice could subject the Company to serious legal consequences, and will result in discipline, up to and including termination.

## Lessons From the Real World

**Destroying email messages can be very costly.**

Laura Zubulake was an equities trader at UBS Warburg. After she was fired, she sued UBS for sex discrimination, failure to promote, and retaliation. During the lawsuit, she asked UBS to hand over email messages that she claimed included biased comments about her by UBS decision makers.

UBS protested that it would cost hundreds of thousands of dollars to retrieve and review its email messages to decide which it had to hand over. The court decided that UBS would have to hand over all relevant messages that were still readily available, but that Zubulake would have to pay part of the estimated cost of restoring backup tapes. Several orders later, it became apparent that some relevant email messages had been deleted after the lawsuit began, against the court's instructions.

The court found that these email messages had been destroyed willfully. As a result, the court ordered UBS to pay some of Zubulake's pretrial costs. More importantly, the court instructed the jury that UBS had destroyed the email messages, and that the jury could conclude that the messages would have been harmful to UBS's case. After hearing all of the evidence as well as this instruction about the missing emails, the jury awarded more than $29 million to Zubulake.

*Zubulake v. UBS Warburg L.L.C.*, 229 F.R.D. 422 (S.D. N.Y. 2004); Eduardo Porter, "UBS Ordered to Pay $29 Million in Sex Bias Lawsuit," *The New York Times*, April 7, 2005.

> ⚠ CAUTION
>
> **Don't forget the acknowledgment form.** If your company adopts the email policy covered in this chapter, make sure you require employees to sign an acknowledgment form. You'll find a sample acknowledgment form and instructions in Appendix B; a blank acknowledgment form is included on the CD-ROM at the back of this book.

# Putting It All Together: Sample Email Policy

Here's a sample email policy for a large financial services company. The company has had some problems with employees sending inappropriate email messages in the past, so it uses software that monitors keywords. It also prohibits all forms of employee solicitation, even for charitable causes. Because many of its employees are relatively new to the work world, the company has decided to adopt the netiquette guidelines as well.

# Email Policy

## Use of the Email System

The email system is intended for official Company business. Although you may use the email system occasionally for personal messages, you may do so during nonworking hours only. If you send personal messages through the Company's email system, you must exercise discretion as to the number and type of messages you send. You must also ensure that your personal use of the email system does not interfere in any way with your job duties or performance. Any employee who abuses this privilege may be subject to discipline.

## Email Is Not Private

Email messages, including attachments, sent and received on Company equipment are the property of the Company. We reserve the right to access, monitor, read, and/or copy email messages at any time, for any reason. You should not expect privacy for any email you send using Company equipment, including messages that you consider to be personal, or label with a designation such as "Personal" or "Private."

In addition, the Company's software automatically searches the messages you send for questionable content, including sexual or racial comments, threats, trade secrets, competitive information, and inappropriate language. Any message deemed questionable will be forwarded to, and read by, Company management.

## All Conduct Rules Apply to Email

All of our policies and rules of conduct apply to employee use of the email system. This means, for example, that you may not use the email system to send harassing or discriminatory messages, including messages with explicit sexual content or pornographic images; to send threatening messages; or to reveal Company trade secrets or confidential information.

### No Solicitation by Email

You may not use the email system to solicit others to patronize an outside business or to support an outside organization, a political candidate or cause, or a religious cause.

### Professional Tone and Content

We expect you to exercise discretion in using electronic communications equipment. When you send email using the Company's equipment, you are representing the Company. Make sure that your messages are professional and appropriate, in tone and content. Remember, although email may seem like a private conversation, email can be printed, saved, and forwarded to unintended recipients. You should not send any email that you wouldn't want your boss, your mother, or our Company's competitors to read.

### Guidelines for Email Writing

1. Always spell-check or proofread your email messages. Email is official Company correspondence. Spelling errors in email are all too common, and they look sloppy and unprofessional.

2. Use lowercase and capital letters in the same way that you would in a letter. Using all capital letters is the email equivalent of shouting at someone—and it can be hard on the eyes. Failing to use capital letters at all (to begin a sentence or formal noun) can confuse readers and seem overly cute. Unless you are writing poetry, use standard capitalization.

3. Remember your audience. Although email encourages informal communication, that might not be the most appropriate style to use if you are addressing the CEO of an important

customer. And, remember that your email can be forwarded to unintended recipients, some of whom may not appreciate joking comments or informalities.

4.  Don't use email for confidential matters. Again, remember the unintended recipient. Your email might be forwarded to someone you didn't anticipate or might be sitting at a printer for all to see. If you need to have a confidential discussion, do it in person or over the phone.

5.  Send messages sparingly. There is rarely a need to copy everyone in the Company on an email. Carefully consider who really needs to see the message, and address it accordingly.

6.  Always think before you send. Resist the urge to respond in anger, to "flame" your recipient, or to get emotional. Although email gives you the opportunity to respond immediately, you don't have to take it.

7.  Don't leave the subject line blank. Always include a brief description, so readers will know what your email is about at a glance. This makes it easier for all of us to manage our email— and makes it more likely that you will receive a response to your message.

8.  Don't overuse the "urgent" tag. Mark a message as urgent only if it is truly important and must be answered right away.

**Email Security**

To avoid email viruses and other threats, employees should not open email attachments from people and businesses they don't recognize, particularly if the email appears to have been forwarded multiple times or has a nonexistent or peculiar subject heading. Even if you know the sender, do not open an email attachment that has a strange name or is not referenced in the body of the email—it may have been transmitted automatically, without the sender's knowledge.

If you believe your computer has been infected by a virus, worm, or other security threat to the Company's system, you must inform the IT department immediately.

Employees also may not share their email passwords with anyone, including coworkers or family members. Revealing passwords to the Company's email system could allow an outsider to access the Company's network.

### Retaining and Deleting Email Messages

Because email messages are electronic records, certain messages must be retained for compliance purposes. Please refer to our record-keeping policy for guidance on which records must be kept, and for how long. If you have any questions about whether and how to retain a particular email message, please ask your manager.

Because of the large volume of emails our Company sends and receives each day, we discourage employees from storing large numbers of email messages that are not subject to the retention rules explained above. Please make a regular practice of deleting email messages once you have read and/or responded to them. If you need to save a particular message, you may print out a paper copy, archive the email, or save it on your hard drive or disk. The Company will purge email messages that have not been archived after 90 days.

The Company may have occasion to suspend our usual rules about deleting email messages (for example, if the Company is involved in a lawsuit requiring it to preserve evidence). If this happens, employees will be notified of the procedures to follow to save email messages. Failing to comply with such a notice could subject the Company to serious legal consequences, and will result in discipline, up to and including termination.

# Internet Use

## In This Chapter:

### Policy Provisions for Employee Internet Use

☐ Personal Use of the Internet

☐ Prohibited Uses of the Internet

☐ No Personal Posts Using Company Equipment

Internet Use Is Not Private:

☐ Alternative 1: Privacy Policy Reserving the Right to Monitor

☐ Alternative 2: Privacy Policy for Companies That Monitor Regularly

☐ Don't Use Personal Email Accounts for Work

Access to Personal Email Accounts:

☐ Alternative 1: No Access to Personal Email Accounts

☐ Alternative 2: Rules for Accessing Personal Email Accounts

☐ Optional Policy Language for Blocking Access to Personal Email

☐ Optional Policy Language for Keylogger Software

t's no wonder that many of us have become blasé about the Internet. It is so ubiquitous, so useful, and so essential to our work that it's hard to believe that we once had to manually track shipments, book travel, locate information, map a trip, or conduct research without it.

As most businesses are aware, however, allowing employees unlimited Internet access poses problems and threats. As a virtual gateway in and out of the company, the Internet tempts employees to spend work time on personal pursuits like shopping, checking sports scores, joining chat rooms, checking their personal email accounts, and even looking for a new job. In addition, employees can use the Internet to access inappropriate material—for example pornography, gambling, and hate speech—which is often deemed offensive by coworkers.

## Where Employees Go Online

According to a 2006 survey by Websense, more than 60% of employees admitted to visiting personal websites at work, for an average of slightly more than three hours total per week. What types of sites did they visit? The most frequented nonwork sites were map sites, followed by news sites and weather sites. Banking, travel, and shopping sites were close behind.

Employee access to the Web can also inadvertently result in damage to the company's computer system and software, from viruses, spyware, and so on. In fact, experts say that more system attacks are launched on companies today via employee Internet surfing than through email.

Finally, the Internet provides a backdoor by which employees can send information out of the company, whether it's transmitting company information through personal email or posting personal comments to outside sites, which can then be traced back to your company.

---

### Do We Have Al Gore to Thank?

Most of the innovations discussed in this book rely on the Internet, known in previous incarnations as the World Wide Web or the Information Superhighway. And we all know who invented the Internet ... or do we?

In the run-up to the 2000 election, Al Gore was said to have claimed that he invented the Internet. But it turns out (1) he never said that, and (2) he wouldn't have been too far wrong if he did.

What Gore actually said, in answering a question from CNN's Wolf Blitzer as to why American voters should choose him over his primary competitor Bill Bradley, was that he "took the initiative in creating the Internet." And so he did: Among many other things, he drafted and sponsored the High Performance Communication and Computing Act of 1991, which led to the National Information Infrastructure and the development of Mosaic, a Web browser many believe to have begun the Internet boom of the 1990s.

Gore later made fun of his statement on *Late Night with David Letterman*, giving as number nine of his top ten list of rejected Gore-Lieberman campaign slogans, "Remember, America, I gave you the Internet and I can take it away!"

---

## Personal Use of the Internet

Banning all personal use of the Internet leads to the same problems—employee resentment, selective enforcement, and so on—as banning all personal email. (See Chapter 3 for more information). A more sensible approach is to allow limited personal use of the Internet during lunch, breaks, or other nonwork hours, as long as that use is not excessive and does not violate the policy's other prohibitions (see "Prohibited Uses of the Internet," below). This will help you not only avoid the problems that an outright ban can create, but also ensure that employees spent more of their work hours doing what your company is actually paying them to do, rather than bidding on eBay auctions or looking for their house on Google Earth.

---

**Personal Use of the Internet**

Our network and Internet access are for official Company business. Employees may access the Internet for personal use only outside of work hours and only in accordance with the other terms of this policy. An employee who engages in excessive Internet use, even during nonwork hours, may be subject to discipline.

---

## After Black Friday Comes Cyber Monday

The day after Thanksgiving has been called "Black Friday," a reference to either the heavy traffic (and ensuing headaches) or the bottom-line profit associated with the biggest shopping day of the year. Those who prefer to shop online apparently do so on "Cyber Monday," the first business day after Thanksgiving, when employees return to their workplace computer terminals.

How much shopping do employees do? Challenger, Gray, and Christmas (an outplacement firm—and yes, that is their real name) estimated that 68 million employees would do some holiday shopping online on Cyber Monday, 2007. If each of those employees spent only 12 minutes shopping, it could cost companies $488 million in lost productivity.

# Prohibited Uses of the Internet

Your policy should tell employees what types of Internet activities and sites are forbidden, what types of downloads and streaming activities are prohibited, and what restrictions the company places on employee postings to other sites.

## Prohibited Sites and Downloads

Start by listing the types of electronic information that employees may not access from work. In addition to banning sites with offensive material (such as pornography and violent images), you should ban two types of downloads: those that violate the law—such as inappropriate use of copyrighted material, stolen music files, unlicensed software programs—or those that could infect your company's system—for example, files that may contain viruses or other system threats.

In addition, your company must also consider its tech capacity limits. Streaming audio or video—for example, Internet radio stations or YouTube—can quickly overload your company's systems and bring the company's Internet connection to a screeching halt. If that's the case at your company, you'll want to add language banning these uses in your policy.

If your company blocks employee access to particular sites or types of sites using a technological solution—for example, filtering software—you should let employees know that their ability to access a site doesn't necessarily mean it's appropriate for viewing. (If your company doesn't use blocking software, simply delete the last paragraph of this section).

**Prohibited Uses of the Internet**

Employees may not, at any time, access the Internet using Company equipment for any of the following purposes:

To view websites that offer pornography, gambling, or violent imagery, or are otherwise inappropriate in the workplace.

To operate an outside business, online auction, or other sales site; solicit money for personal purposes; or to otherwise act for personal financial gain or profit.

To download or copy software, games, text, photos, or any other works in violation of copyright, trademark, or other laws.

To stream, run, or download any non-Company-licensed software program without the express consent of the IT department.

To stream, run, or download music, video, games, minidesktop applications (widgets), or any form of multimedia, from the Internet.

To read, open, or download any file from the Internet without first screening that file for viruses using the Company's virus detection software.

If you believe that your job may require you to do something that would otherwise be forbidden by this policy, ask your manager how to proceed.

To assure that employees comply with this policy, we use software that will block your access to many prohibited sites. However, some inappropriate websites may escape detection by the software: The fact that you can access a particular site does not necessarily mean that site is appropriate for workplace viewing.

## Lessons From the Real World

### Is Internet sex addiction a disability?

James Pacenza worked for IBM for 19 years until he was fired after a coworker witnessed a chatroom discussion about sex on Pacenza's computer screen. Pacenza claimed that his termination was illegal because, among other things, he visited Internet chat rooms as a way to "self-medicate" his disability.

Pacenza, a veteran of the Vietnam War, suffered from post-traumatic stress disorder and depression. Pacenza claimed that IBM shouldn't have fired him because Internet sex addiction was a manifestation of his disability. Therefore, the company's decision to fire him—rather than working with him to come up with a reasonable accommodation—was discriminatory.

Not surprisingly, IBM contended that Pacenza was fired for violating its policy on Internet misuse, and that it had no obligation to accommodate his desire to engage in sexual chatroom discussions.

Pacenza's case hasn't been decided yet, and there are no reported cases, to date, on Internet addiction as a disability, whether the claimed addiction is to the Internet itself (for someone who can't be offline for more than a few hours or can't stop checking email) or to the Internet's ability to bring other addictive material directly to the user (for example, porn sites for a sex addict or gaming sites for a gambling addict). But that probably won't last forever. Today, you can find therapists who specialize in treating Internet addiction, scholarly articles on the problem, and even 12-step programs to combat the addiction (ironically, some are available online).

Even if Internet sex addiction becomes a legally recognized disability, however, employers who utilize blocking software have little to worry about: One proposed "reasonable accommodation" is to make sure that employees can't access inappropriate sites—particularly porn sites—while at work, which is exactly what blocking software is designed to accomplish.

## Prohibited Posts to Other Sites

When employees state their personal opinions by, for example, posting a comment to a blog or forum, those opinions could mistakenly be attributed to their employer—for example, if the employee or the employee's email address gives it away. In addition, any transmission may be traceable back to your company computers (or to an Internet Protocol address—a unique number that points to your company as the source). This can lead to trouble if the employee posts something controversial. To avoid this danger, your policy should prohibit employees from posting to other sites using company equipment. (For information on employee posts from personal computers to blogs, websites, or third-party sites, see Chapter 6.)

---

**No Personal Posts Using Company Equipment**

Employees should not use the Company's equipment to transmit their personal opinions by, for example, posting a comment to a blog or contributing to an online forum. Even if you don't identify yourself as a Company employee, your opinion could be mistaken for the Company's view.

---

**Lessons From the Real World**

**To the virtual barricades! When avatars strike.**

Apparently, the Hollywood writers' strike wasn't the only work stoppage in the Fall of 2007: Italian employees of IBM also went on strike. At least, their avatars did—in Second Life.

Second Life (www.secondlife.com) is a virtual world in which real people and real companies can role play—that is, maintain a virtual presence with visual representations (avatars) and real estate. For example, IBM, like many businesses, maintains its own "campus" or "island" within the Second Life environment.

According to press reports, the trade union representing IBM's workers in Italy requested a pay increase and IBM responded by cutting performance bonuses. The union then solicited a virtual strike by Second Lifers; it asked Residents to man the picket lines and occupy IBM's Second Life real estate.

This virtual occupation—over 1,800 Residents stormed the IBM campus—must have had some success. Talks with the union resumed, the performance bonuses were reinstated, and the person responsible for the pay cuts resigned. And here's a benefit you don't see from most strikes: Strike organizers won a "NetXplorateur" prize in 2008 from the French Senate, intended to recognize the most exemplary Web-related projects of the year.

# Privacy

Just as you did in your email policy, you should tell employees that their Internet use is not private. A policy like this—whether you currently monitor employee Internet usage or just want to reserve the right in the future—may greatly minimize your company's legal exposure.

Here are some examples of situations when you might need to investigate an employee's Internet activity:

- Several employees complain that their manager is viewing pornography on his computer terminal. They claim that the manager has offensive pictures up on his screen when he calls them into his office for meetings or conversations. The manager denies everything.

- Posts to several online investor forums indicate that a publicly traded company will soon release a new product, resulting in a quick jump in its stock price. A few members of the company's management team sell off much of their stock shortly before the rumor is shown to be false.

- An employee's performance has declined significantly, and coworkers claim that he spends most of his time trying to accumulate friends on his MySpace page. The employee claims that his job requires him to check social networking sites, such as MySpace and Facebook, to see what job applicants have posted about themselves, but he doesn't access those sites from work for personal reasons.

If your company uses monitoring software (according to a 2005 survey, more than ¾ of employers do), you should let employees know. After all, the goal is not just to keep track of where employees go on the Internet, but to stop them from going to inappropriate sites in the first place. Telling employees that they're being watched is sure to cut down on prohibited, unnecessary, and unauthorized surfing.

The first policy, below, simply reserves the right to monitor. The second version tells employees that monitoring is underway.

### Alternative 1: Privacy Policy Reserving the Right to Monitor

**Internet Use Is Not Private**

We reserve the right to monitor employee use of the Internet at any time. You should not expect that your use of the Internet— including but not limited to the sites you visit, the amount of time you spend online, and the communications you have—will be private.

### Alternative 2: Privacy Policy for Companies That Monitor Regularly

**Internet Use Is Not Private**

Our Company uses monitoring software that, among other things, tracks the sites an employee visits and how much time is spent at a particular site. You should not expect that your use of the Internet— including but not limited to the sites you visit, the amount of time you spend online, and the communications you have—will be private.

# Personal Web-based Email

Although most companies have policies that address use of the company's email system (see Chapter 3), many companies have no policy regarding employees accessing their personal email accounts from work. At first blush, it might seem like overkill to limit an employee's ability to check a personal email account from work. After all, if the company doesn't want employees to send a lot of personal messages on its own system, shouldn't it allow them to access their own accounts, at least during breaks and lunch?

Unfortunately, it's not that simple. Personal email accounts, such as those available from Hotmail, Yahoo!, Comcast, and AOL, are Web-based. When an employee accesses this type of account from work, messages sent and received bypass the employer's security system. This means bad things—such as viruses, Trojan horses, and spyware—can get in, and good things—like trade secrets—can get out, and the company will never know about it.

## Doing Business Via Personal Email

Even employees with the best intentions can create huge problems for a company via their personal email accounts. Take, for example, the common practice of employees sending work-related documents or messages to their personal email address. Most employees who do this are simply trying to make it easier to work from home; some are trying to get around an employer system that allows them to save only a limited number of messages by keeping those messages in their personal account. And still other employees automatically forward messages they receive at work to their personal account, to make sure they can access their email while traveling for business. What harm could that cause?

Plenty, as it turns out. Those work documents and messages are stored not on the company's servers but on the Internet, where they could potentially be accessed by people outside the company. What if the employee's ISP scans messages to send targeted advertising to the user? What if someone hacks into the ISP's servers? What if the employee's laptop is stolen, with a saved password that allows the thief easy access to the employee's Web-based account? This is especially problematic if the forwarded information is something the employer has an obligation to keep private, such as medical records, customer information, or company trade secrets.

Beyond the potential theft or exposure of company records, allowing employees to transact company business via their personal email accounts creates another big problem for the company: Some of its business records are out of its control. The company might not even know about key negotiations, discussions, and deals that are carried out on personal email. It won't have those records if it needs to recreate contract talks, review an employee's personnel file, or respond to a subpoena. And, employees may save documents long after they would have been purged from the company's records, which means there could be a "smoking gun" out there that could have been destroyed.

All companies should adopt a policy prohibiting employees from using their personal email accounts to transact company business. This includes not only using those accounts for business correspondence, but also transmitting any messages or files that might contain confidential information.

---

**Don't Use Personal Email Accounts for Work**

Employees may not use their own personal email accounts to transact Company business. This includes storing work-related documents and email messages in your personal email account, sending work to your personal email account, engaging in work-related communications (with customers, clients, or coworkers, for example) using your personal email account, or "bouncing" messages from your Company email to your personal email when you are out of the office.

Although employees may find these practices convenient, they can create significant security problems, expose confidential Company information, and compromise the Company's record-keeping obligations. If you work offsite (for example, at home or on business travel), please contact the IT department to find out how to safely transmit and protect Company information.

---

## Accessing Personal Email Accounts at Work

The risks discussed above give employers very good reasons to simply prohibit employees from using their Web-based email accounts at work. However, many companies are uncomfortable with a total ban. Surveys show that one-half to three-quarters of responding companies have no policies on access to Web-based email. Some are probably unaware of the potential problems; others may simply think a policy banning employee access to their own email accounts is too Draconian.

Your company will have to decide, based on its culture, level of trust in its employees, and values, whether to adopt a total ban. Even if your company decides not to prohibit all access to personal email, however, it should still have a policy putting some limits on the practice.

### Alternative 1: Banning Access to Personal Email

**No Access to Personal Email**

Accessing your personal email account from work creates security risks for the Company's computer system and network. Therefore, employees may not use Company equipment to access their personal email accounts.

**Alternative 2: Allowing Access to Personal Email**

---

**Rules for Accessing Personal Email**

Accessing your personal email account from work creates security risks for the Company's computer system and network. To help control these risks, employees must follow these rules when using Company equipment to access their personal email:

You may access your personal email account during nonwork hours only.

Do not open any personal email messages from an unknown sender. Personal email is subject only to the security controls imposed by your provider, which may be less strict than the Company's. If a personal message contains a virus or other malware, it could infect the Company's network.

Before you open any attachment, you must scan it for viruses using the Company's antivirus software.

You may not transact Company business using your personal email account, nor may you transmit any Company documents using your personal email account.

---

## Monitoring or Blocking Personal Email

If your company decides to ban employee access to their personal email accounts, you can use blocking software to prevent employees from accessing common email sites such as Hotmail, Yahoo!, and so on. If your company's monitoring system allows it to see employee messages in their personal email accounts (for example, because you use software that tracks everything the employee types or captures a screenshot of employee computers), you should let employees know.

The exact language you put in your policy will depend on the type of monitoring or blocking tools your company uses. Here are a couple of examples:

**Optional Policy Language for Blocking Access
to Personal Web-based Email Sites:**

> The Company's security software blocks access to many Web-based email sites. The fact that you can access a Web-based email site does not mean that you are free to check personal email using the Company's equipment, however.

**Optional Policy Language for Keylogger Software:**

> The Company's monitoring software keeps track of everything you type on your computer. Therefore, although the Company allows employees to access their personal email accounts using Company equipment, employees should not expect any messages they send or view from work to be private. The Company can access and read these messages at any time, even if they are designated as "personal" or "private."

> **CAUTION**
>
> **Don't forget the acknowledgment form.** If your company adopts the Internet policy covered in this chapter, make sure you require employees to sign an acknowledgment form. You'll find a sample acknowledgment form and instructions in Appendix B; a blank acknowledgment form is included on the CD-ROM at the back of this book.

## Putting It All Together: Sample Internet Policy

Here's a sample Internet use policy adopted by an independent bookstore. Employees need Internet access occasionally to answer customer questions, but don't spend much time online. The store doesn't have the time, money, or staff to actively monitor employee Internet use, nor has it invested in monitoring or blocking software. Because it also has limited IT capability, the store has decided to simply prohibit employees from accessing inappropriate sites, downloading or streaming improper materials, participating in outside business ventures, making personal posts, or accessing their personal email accounts from work.

# Using the Internet

## Personal Use of the Internet

Our network and Internet access are for official Company business. Employees may access the Internet for personal use only outside of work hours and only in accordance with the other terms of this policy. An employee who engages in excessive Internet use, even during nonwork hours, may be subject to discipline.

## Prohibited Uses of the Internet

Employees may not, at any time, access the Internet using Company equipment for any of the following purposes:

To view websites that offer pornography, gambling, or violent imagery, or are otherwise inappropriate in the workplace.

To operate an outside business, online auction, or other sales site; solicit money for personal purposes; or to otherwise act for personal financial gain or profit.

To download or copy software, games, text, photos, or any other works in violation of copyright, trademark, or other laws.

To stream, run, or download any non-Company-licensed software program without the express consent of the IT department.

To stream, run, or download music, video, games, minidesktop applications (widgets), or any form of multimedia, from the Internet.

To read, open, or download any file from the Internet without first screening that file for viruses using the Company's virus detection software.

If you believe that your job may require you to do something that would otherwise be forbidden by this policy, ask your manager how to proceed.

### No Personal Posts Using Company Equipment

Employees should not use the Company's equipment to transmit their personal opinions by, for example, posting a comment to a blog or contributing to an online forum. Even if you don't identify yourself as a Company employee, your opinion could be mistaken for the Company's view.

### Internet Use Is Not Private

We reserve the right to monitor employee use of the Internet at any time. You should not expect that your use of the Internet—including but not limited to the sites you visit, the amount of time you spend online, and the communications you have—will be private.

### Don't Use Personal Email Accounts for Work

Employees may not use their own personal email accounts to transact Company business. This includes storing work-related documents and email messages in your personal email account, sending work to your personal email account, engaging in work-related communications (with customers, clients, or coworkers, for example) using your personal email account, or "bouncing" messages from your Company email to your personal email when you are out of the office.

Although employees may find these practices convenient, they can create significant security problems, expose confidential Company information, and compromise the Company's record-keeping obligations. If you work offsite (for example, at home or on business travel), please contact the IT department to find out how to safely transmit and protect Company information.

### No Access to Personal Email

Accessing your personal email account from work creates security risks for the Company's computer system and network. Therefore, employees may not use Company equipment to access their personal email accounts.

# Instant Messaging

## In This Chapter:

### Policy Provisions for Instant Messaging

☐ Alternative 1: No Instant Messaging

☐ Alternative 2: No Use of Consumer Instant Messaging

☐ Alternative 3: Using Consumer Instant Messaging Software

☐ IM Usernames and Passwords

☐ Personal Use of IM

☐ IM Is Not Private

☐ All Conduct Rules Apply to IM

☐ IM Security

☐ Retaining and Deleting Instant Messages

I nstant messaging ("IM") is a form of text-based real-time communication. Users operate a software program (referred to as a "client"), which allows them to see who else in their IM network (often called a "buddy list" or "contact list") is online. The user can initiate a conversation with an online contact by sending a message, which triggers a pop-up window on the contact's computer. If the contact responds, a running dialog unfolds on the screen until the conversation ends. All instant messages travel though a server operated by the IM company—for example, when you use America Online Instant Messenger (AIM), all of your text passes through AOL's servers.

IM comes primarily in three flavors:

**Consumer Instant Messaging.** This is the wildly successful version of IM, first popularized by AOL's AIM system. (AOL's parent company owns the trademark "Instant Messenger.") Competing IM systems include Yahoo Messenger, Jabber, Google Messenger, and MSN Messenger. These commercial IMs are easy-to-use, feature friendly graphic interfaces, and are generally incompatible with each other (attempts to standardize IM protocols have failed so far).

**Enterprise Instant Messaging (EIM).** EIM systems are designed for business use and include the security and legal requirements needed by corporate IT departments. Leading providers include Microsoft, IBM Lotus, and Jabber. Some systems are designed to be industry-specific—for example, Reuters provides IM systems for the financial services industry. EIMs can also incorporate users of consumer IMs such as AOL, Yahoo, and MSN.

**Mobile Instant Messaging (MIM).** MIM is simply instant messaging in motion. Modern cellular phones and PDAs come with some IM capability, sometimes also referred to as a Short Message Service (or SMS). In addition, many mobile devices are capable of running third party IM software. For example, the popular BlackBerry can run more than 15 instant message programs including mobile versions of Yahoo, MSN, and AOL's IM programs.

Should you allow employees to use IM? If so, will you allow them to use commercial IM software or require them to use an EIM system licensed by the company? What limits—on personal use and content, for example—will you place on employee use of IM? And how will you make sure that important messages transmitted via IM will be saved and available when the company needs them? This chapter explains your company's policy options.

## To IM or Not to IM?

IM is a great medium for quick, vital correspondence, such as "contract signed," "shipment didn't arrive this a.m.," or "original order sold out; please send 1,000 additional units ASAP." For that reason, certain business that rely on speed—stock trading and sales are two obvious examples—have quickly adopted IM systems in order to connect the right people, right away.

There are other potential IM benefits for businesses, as well. For example, business users of IM can see who's logged in and immediately direct important questions or concerns to an appropriate person who can handle them quickly. In addition, employees who work offsite can use IM to interact more directly with coworkers than they could by phone or email. And, IM allows employees to multitask: IM software is intended to run in the background, so employees can do other work while still receiving and responding to important instant messages. IM also helps many companies perform more efficiently by eliminating telephone tag, email bounce messages, and even some of the need for business travel.

## IM May Increase Productivity

IM can be a distraction for employees. The message notification feature—which shows up on top of everything else on your screen—can be disruptive, and the fact that others know you are online can invite conversations for which you really don't have time. So, you may be surprised to learn that a recent survey showed that employees who use IM report fewer workplace interruptions than those who don't.

Almost 30% of those who responded to the survey used IM at work; interestingly, employees between the ages of 46 and 55 were most likely to do so. IM users were less likely to agree with the statement, "I rarely complete a work task without being interrupted," than nonusers. The survey also found that using IM doesn't increase an employee's overall communication time—in other words, IM replaces other forms of communication rather than adding to them.

R. Kelly Garrett and James N. Danziger, "IM=Interruption Management? Instant Messaging and Disruption in the Workplace," *Journal of Computer-Mediated Communication* 13(1) (2007).

As is true of the other technological innovations covered in this book, however, these advantages don't come without some concerns. Among them are:

- **Security risks.** IM systems can carry files, and hackers have learned how to exploit this feature—particularly on commercial IM systems—to infect users' machines. Once one machine is infected, the malware is usually programmed to propagate by transmitting itself to everyone on the user's contact list. Unlike typical contagions by email which take a day or two, IM virus infections spread in hours.

- **Loss of proprietary information.** As with all forms of communication, IM enables employees to quickly pass your company's proprietary information to third parties. In addition, unless you have a purely internal EIM system, all IMs travel via public third party servers.

- **Messaging spam (spim).** Just in case your business is not getting enough unsolicited commercial messages, IMs can bring you more of the same—except now it's *instant*.

- **Archiving.** Although some EIMs come with built-in archiving, many consumer IM systems do not automatically archive exchanges (as is done with email). As a result, your company may not be able to produce requested IM documents in a lawsuit.

- **Loss of productivity.** Anyone who has used IM knows it can be a tremendous time sink. And unfortunately, because of the way IM works, it can be hard for the well-mannered to ignore that little pop-up window saying "how RU?" Most of us feel we have to respond at the risk of being rude.

- **Informality.** Something about the format of IM—and the fact that it was developed for use in chatrooms—makes users feel that it's strictly for informal social conversation. This can lead to a lack of professionalism in business-related IM, and to inappropriate jokes, comments, or gossip.

### Beyond Informality ... the Saga of Maf54

In one of the most shocking tales of workplace misuse of IM, Mark Foley, the former Republican Congressman from Florida, resigned in 2006 after his sexual communications with former male pages—several of whom had saved the heated IM dialogs—became public.

Foley, identified as "Maf54," called one of the correspondents his "favorite young stud," told the former page he was picturing his "great legs" and "cute butt," and soon was into unprintable territory. (At the same time that these conversations were going on, Foley was also the Chairman of the House Caucus on Missing and Exploited Children, which introduced legislation targeting sexual predators.) Foley initially claimed that the messages he sent were innocuous and accused his opponent of dirty politics. Once several news sources printed excerpts from the saved IMs, Foley apologized and immediately resigned.

## Alternative 1: Prohibiting IM

The initial decision your company must make is whether IM—either a commercial or enterprise system—has any place in your business. As you consider your company's options, remember that many of your employees are probably already using IM on their work computers. As a practical matter, this means that banning or placing strict limits on IM amounts to taking away something employees already have—which is much more difficult than preventing them from using it in the first place.

If you wish to halt current use (and future uses), your company must block downloads of consumer IM software and routinely audit employee computers to make sure they aren't breaking the rules. Banning IM may also limit your company's options in communicating with future clients, customers, suppliers, and business partners.

If your company nonetheless decides to ban IM altogether—perhaps your employees don't need to correspond in real time, you have no or very few employees who work remotely, and your customers and clients don't expect your employees to be available via IM—you can use the policy language below. (You can also skip the rest of this chapter, which applies only to companies that have decided to allow IM in some form.)

---

**No Instant Messaging**

Because of the security risks associated with publicly available IM software, instant messaging is prohibited at our Company. Employees may not download or use personal IM software from the Internet to send or receive instant messages. For example, employees may not use Yahoo! Messenger, AOL Instant Messenger, Windows Live Messenger, or Google Chat. Violation of this policy will result in discipline, up to and including termination.

# Permitting IM

If your company decides against an outright IM ban, it has two primary options: It can allow IM only through its own enterprise software or it can allow employees to use consumer IM software.

## Alternative 2: Allowing IM Via Enterprise Software

Using enterprise IM software allows your company to avoid some of the problems associated with publicly available IM systems. Your company controls the system, so it can monitor content, check for viruses and other malware, and control abuse. A company-wide IM system can also automatically save and store IM dialogs. And, because all employees will be on the same IM system, you won't face any compatibility problems. On the other hand, enterprise software generally lacks some of the flexibility associated with consumer IM—in particular, employees can only communicate with each other, not the outside world.

Still, an enterprise IM system is ideal for intracompany communications. If your company goes this route, it may also want to prohibit employees from using consumer IM systems. After all, most of the benefits of using a company system will be lost if you leave the back door open.

---

**No Use of Consumer Instant Messaging Systems**

To facilitate communication among employees, our Company has an internal instant messaging (IM) system.

Because of the security risks associated with publicly available IM software, employees may not download or use personal IM software from the Internet to send or receive instant messages. For example, employees may not use Yahoo! Messenger, AOL Instant Messenger, Windows Live Messenger, or Google Chat. Violation of this policy will result in discipline, up to and including termination.

---

### Alternative 3: Allowing IM Via Consumer IM Software

For most companies, especially those with significant numbers of tech-savvy employees, a common solution is to allow employees to (continue to) use consumer IM software and manage the attendant risks using gateway software—software that allows your company to monitor incoming and outgoing IM, scan messages for content and viruses, and archive IM conversations. If you choose this option, you should require employees to utilize your IT department for installation and maintenance of consumer IMs.

---

**Using Consumer Instant Messaging Software**

Our Company makes instant messaging (IM) capability available to our employees. If you wish to use IM, you must notify the IT department and let them know which publicly available IM software you would like to use. The IT department will download the appropriate software and set up your IM account.

Employees may not download or use any IM software on their own, without going through the IT department. Violation of this policy will result in discipline, up to and including termination.

---

# Usernames

There's a reason most people sending IMs aren't using the names listed on their birth certificates: Their screen names allow them to operate behind a pseudonym, to make a statement or to just illustrate a sense of humor.

This is all well and good behind the closed doors of home, but your company really doesn't want its clients receiving business-related IM from babealicious10 or lostfan1. If you allow employees to use IM, you'll need to make sure they adopt professional, straight-forward usernames.

---

**IM Usernames and Passwords**

Employees will be assigned an IM user ID and password by the
IT department. Employees may not change their user ID without
permission.

If you have a personal account with any IM software provider, you
may not use Company equipment to access your personal account.
You may use only the ID and password provided by the Company.

---

## Personal Use of IM

Will your company limit IM to business use only, or will you
permit personal use as well? Banning all personal use of IM has
its risks, chief among them that your company will inconsistently
enforce that ban. Employees who are disciplined for instant messaging conduct (while others get away with it) may claim that your
company engaged in retaliation, discrimination, or unfair labor
practices. (See Chapter 3 for more information on the dangers of
adopting a rule that isn't consistently enforced.) The better practice,
as is true of email, is to allow some personal use of IM. The sample
policy language below echoes the personal use policy for email from
Chapter 3.

**Personal Use of IM**

The IM system is intended for official Company business. Although you may send occasional personal instant messages, you may do so during nonwork hours only. If you send personal messages through the Company's IM system, you must exercise discretion as to the number and type of messages you send. You must also ensure that your personal use of IM does not interfere in any way with your job duties or performance. Any employee who abuses this privilege may be subject to discipline.

## Lessons From the Real World

**Instant messages on employee's work computer lead to search of home computer.**

Brian Toon was the vice president of technology solutions at Quotient Inc. until October 31, 2005. In December 2005, Quotient sued Toon for breach of contract and interference with contractual relations, among other things. Quotient claimed that Toon allowed a former Quotient employee access to Quotient's computer system, trade secrets, and other proprietary information, so the former employee could compete against Quotient.

Almost immediately after filing the lawsuit, Quotient asked the judge to allow it to copy the contents of Toon's home computer. Quotient argued that it had discovered evidence on Toon's work computer, including instant messages in which Toon and the former employee discussed competing against Quotient. Quotient also claimed that it had discovered emails and IMs indicating that Toon was using his personal email account and home computer for similar discussions. Quotient asked the court to allow an expert to copy the contents of Toon's home computer, to make sure that no evidence was inadvertently destroyed or overwritten before the court could decide whether Toon would have to hand it over.

Toon opposed the motion, claiming that copying his home computer would invade his and his wife's privacy. Despite this argument, the court allowed his computer to be copied but not reviewed. If the court later determined that Quotient was entitled to view any of the contents, they could be reviewed by Toon's lawyer, so any private, privileged, or otherwise unrelated material could be withheld.

*Quotient Inc v. Toon*, Case No. 13-C-05-64087 (Md. Cir. Ct. 2005).

# Privacy and IM Monitoring

Like your email policy, your IM policy must inform employees that their instant messages are not private, and it must reserve the company's right to monitor and read IMs at any time. Even if your company doesn't currently read employee IM, it may one day have to do so if an employee is accused of sending sexually harassing messages, transmitting trade secrets to a competitor, or using IM to spread false rumors about another employee, for example.

As discussed in Chapter 3, the key to successfully defending against an employee's invasion of privacy claim is to tell employees explicitly that their messages are not private. This is especially important in the context of IM, which seems so ephemeral. (Once the dialog box disappears from the screen, many employees mistakenly assume that it's gone forever and, therefore, can't be retrieved or read by their employer.) Knowing that IM will be read also provides a powerful deterrent to inappropriate content.

What your policy should say about monitoring depends on how your monitoring software works. If, for example, your company uses "keylogger" software that tracks everything an employee types, you should put that information in your policy. If your company uses gateway software that scans outgoing IM for questionable content, you should add that to your policy. You can find sample monitoring policy language in Chapter 3.

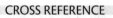 CROSS REFERENCE

**Deciding whether to regularly monitor employee communications can be a very tough call.** This is especially true for companies that have positioned themselves, internally or externally, as creative, pro-employee, or simply as a "fun" place to work. For information on the pros and cons of monitoring, see Chapter 3.

**IM Is Not Private**

Instant messages sent and received on Company equipment are the property of the Company. We reserve the right to access, monitor, read, and/or copy instant messages at any time, for any reason. You should not expect that IM you send using Company equipment— including messages that you consider to be, or label as, personal— will be private.

## Lessons From the Real World

**Employee's IM might be private if employer said it wouldn't read the messages.**

Jeff Quon was a sergeant on the SWAT team of Ontario, California. He received a pager with wireless text-messaging capability for work, and was told that the department's email policy applied to use of the pagers. That policy said that personal use was a significant policy violation; that the city had the right to monitor all activity; that users should not expect privacy; and that obscene or suggestive messages were prohibited.

However, there was also an informal policy that applied to the pagers. The lieutenant in charge of administering employee use of the pagers told employees that each pager was allotted 25,000 characters per month, and that he would not audit their pagers as long as they paid any overage charges each month. The department did not audit anyone's pager messages for the first eight months after the pagers were issued.

Quon exceeded the character limit three or four times, and paid the overage each time. When Quon and another officer again went over the limit, the chief decided that the messages sent and received on certain pagers (including Quon's) should be audited to figure out whether the city should increase the number of allowed characters and whether the officers were using the pagers for personal reasons. Because the city could not access the messages themselves, it asked its carrier (Arch Wireless) to provide transcripts. Those transcripts revealed that many of Quon's messages were personal and some were sexually explicit. Quon, his wife, and two other people with whom he exchanged text messages sued for violation of their rights to privacy.

The 9th Circuit Court of Appeals found that the city had violated their privacy rights. Despite the written policy, the court found that the lieutenant's statement that he would not read their messages, combined with his practice of actually not reading messages for months, created a reasonable expectation of privacy. The court also found that, although the city's purpose of figuring out whether it should pay for more characters was reasonable, it didn't have to read employee messages to achieve that goal. For example, it could have warned Quon in advance that his pager would be audited after the date of the notice, asked Quon to redact the personal messages, or asked Quon to count the work-related characters himself.

*Quon v. Arch Wireless Operating Co.*, 529 F.3d 892 (9th Cir. 2008).

## Inappropriate Content Rules

As email and IM have become more popular, they have also become vehicles for inappropriate conduct. The potential content problems your company might encounter in IM are essentially the same as it might find in email: harassment, inappropriate jokes and comments, solicitations for various causes or businesses, lack of professionalism, and so on. In fact, the extremely informal nature of IM makes it even more vulnerable to these types of problems.

If your company has adopted IM in some form, then you should make clear that your company's conduct rules apply with full force to IM.

**All Conduct Rules Apply to IM**

All of our policies and rules of conduct apply to employee use of instant messaging (IM). This means, for example, that you may not use IM to send harassing or discriminatory messages, including messages with explicit sexual content or pornographic images; to send threatening messages; or to reveal Company trade secrets or confidential information.

## Lessons From the Real World

**Employee fired for IM message claims that he was reporting harassment.**

Todd Bernier was fired from his job as an equities analyst at Morningstar, Inc., for sending an instant message to a coworker, Christopher Davis. Bernier felt that Davis, who is gay, had sexually harassed him by staring at his private parts while both were using the urinal. (During the litigation, it came out that Davis has a "lazy eye" that sometimes makes it appear that he's looking at something else while conversing.) Rather than using the company's harassment complaint process, Bernier sent an anonymous IM to Davis through the company's internal system, saying "Stop staring! The guys on the floor don't like it."

Unlike Bernier, Davis did use the company's complaint process—to claim that he had been sexually harassed. The company investigated. When questioned, Bernier denied sending the IM; he was fired several hours later. At the termination meeting, Bernier admitted sending the IM and explained why he did so. Bernier later sued Morningstar for sexual harassment and retaliation.

Bernier lost on both claims. The court found no evidence that the company knew he was claiming harassment. He didn't use the company's complaint process, sent the IM anonymously to a coworker, and then denied sending it. Even after Davis brought the IM to the company's attention, there was no reason for the company to infer that the sender of the IM—as opposed to the recipient—felt sexually harassed.

*Bernier v. Morningstar, Inc.*, 495 F.3d 369 (7th Cir. 2007).

# Viruses and Security Threats

IM can be especially vulnerable to viruses, worms, and bots because of the way these threats travel. Unlike spam, which often has a nonsensical subject line and is sent from an unknown source, IM malware looks like an actual message from someone known to the recipient. Once an IM security threat infects one person's account, it typically sends itself to everyone on that person's buddy list within hours. A buddy who opens the message or downloads an attached file then becomes the next infectious agent. If you have permitted IM in your company, you should adopt the policy below.

**IM Security**

To avoid viruses and other threats, employees should not open instant messages or file attachments from people and businesses they don't recognize. Even if you know the sender, do not open an IM attachment that has a strange name or is not referenced in the body of the IM—it may have been transmitted automatically, without the sender's knowledge.

If you believe your computer has been infected by a virus, worm, or other security threat to the Company's system, you must inform the IT department immediately.

Employees may not share their IM password with anyone, nor may they use another employee's IM account.

# Retention and Deletion

Like email messages, instant messages are electronic records. This means not only that your company may have a need, or an obligation, to retain some of these records, but also that these documents may be subject to discovery in a lawsuit. IMs are probably less likely to contain important information that your company needs to keep, simply because instant messaging doesn't lend itself to formal correspondence (for example, job applications, contract negotiations, or performance feedback). Most IMs your company generates can safely be deleted once the conversation ends.

For those few IMs that may have to be retained, your policy should explain how employees can save them. (And, at the same time, your company should institute training procedures so that employees understand how to retain and archive such messages.) It should also explain that other IMs—those that the company isn't obligated to keep—should be deleted once they are dealt with.

---

### Retaining and Deleting Instant Messages

Because instant messages are electronic records, certain IMs must be retained for compliance purposes. Please refer to our record-keeping policy for guidance on which records must be kept, and for how long. If you have any questions about whether and how to retain a particular IM, please ask your manager.

We discourage employees from storing instant messages that are not subject to the retention rules explained above. Please make a regular practice of deleting IMs once you have read and/or responded to them. If you need to save a particular message, you may print out a paper copy, archive the message, or save it on your hard drive or disk. The Company will purge IMs that have not been archived after _____ days.

---

## Some IM Slang—HTH!

Emails, text messaging, and particularly IMs, have helped to create a new slanguage with terms such as LOL (laughing out loud) or BFF (best friends forever). Many of these terms are simple acronyms; some use the sound of letters and numbers to create words (such as L8R for "later" or NE1 for "anyone"). Here are some of the more common (that don't include curse words):

AFAIK: as far as I know

AFK: away from keyboard

BTDT: been there, done that

CU: see you

EOM: end of message

FWIW: for what it's worth

HAND: have a nice day

HTH: hope this/that helps

IANAL: I am not a lawyer

IMHO: in my humble opinion

IYKWIM: if you know what I mean

j/k: just kidding

MYOB: mind your own business

NSFW: not safe for work

OMG: oh my god

OTOH: on the other hand

SCNR: sorry, could not resist

TBH: to be honest

TMI: too much information

TTFN: ta ta for now

WRT: with respect to

YW: you're welcome

CAUTION

**Don't forget the acknowledgment form.** If your company adopts the instant messaging policy covered in this chapter, make sure you require employees to sign an acknowledgment form. You'll find a sample acknowledgment form and instructions in Appendix B; a blank acknowledgment form is included on the CD-ROM at the back of this book.

# Putting It All Together: A Sample Instant Messaging Policy

Here's a sample IM policy adopted by a company with a large sales force. The company decides to allow use of consumer IM to facilitate communication between salespeople and their customers. Salespeople are paid on commission, so the company isn't too worried about them wasting time on personal IM. As a result, it has decided not to monitor IM, but only to reserve its right to do so.

# Instant Messaging Policy

## Using Consumer Instant Messaging Software

Our Company makes instant messaging (IM) capability available to our employees. If you wish to use IM, you must notify the IT department and let them know which publicly available IM software you would like to use. The IT department will download the appropriate software and set up your IM account.

Employees may not download or use any IM software on their own, without going through the IT department. Violation of this policy will result in discipline, up to and including termination.

## IM Usernames and Passwords

Employees will be assigned an IM user ID and password by the IT department. Employees may not change their user ID without permission.

If you have a personal account with any IM software provider, you may not use Company equipment to access your personal account. You may use only the ID and password provided by the Company.

## Personal Use of IM

The IM system is intended for official Company business. Although you may send occasional personal instant messages, you may do so during nonwork hours only. If you send personal messages through the Company's IM system, you must exercise discretion as to the number and type of messages you send. You must also ensure that your personal use of IM does not interfere in any way with your job duties or performance. Any employee who abuses this privilege may be subject to discipline.

### IM Is Not Private

Instant messages sent and received on Company equipment are the property of the Company. We reserve the right to access, monitor, read, and/or copy instant messages at any time, for any reason. You should not expect that IM you send using Company equipment—including messages that you consider to be, or label as, personal—will be private.

### All Conduct Rules Apply to IM

All of our policies and rules of conduct apply to employee use of instant messaging (IM). This means, for example, that you may not use IM to send harassing or discriminatory messages, including messages with explicit sexual content or pornographic images; to send threatening messages; or to reveal Company trade secrets or confidential information.

### IM Security

To avoid viruses and other threats, employees should not open instant messages or file attachments from people and businesses they don't recognize. Even if you know the sender, do not open an IM attachment that has a strange name or is not referenced in the body of the IM—it may have been transmitted automatically, without the sender's knowledge.

If you believe your computer has been infected by a virus, worm, or other security threat to the Company's system, you must inform the IT department immediately.

Employees may not share their IM password with anyone, nor may they use another employee's IM account.

### Retaining and Deleting Instant Messages

Because instant messages are electronic records, certain IMs must be retained for compliance purposes. Please refer to our record-keeping policy for guidance on which records must be kept, and for how long. If you have any questions about whether and how to retain a particular IM, please ask your manager.

We discourage employees from storing instant messages that are not subject to the retention rules explained above. Please make a regular practice of deleting IMs once you have read and/or responded to them. If you need to save a particular message, you may print out a paper copy, archive the message, or save it on your hard drive or disk. The Company will purge IMs that have not been archived after 90 days.

# Blogs and Beyond:
# Personal Posting on the Internet

*In This Chapter:*

## Policy Provisions for Blogs and Personal Postings

☐ Personal Blogs and Online Posts

☐ No Posting Using Company Resources

☐ Guidelines for Blogs and Online Posts

Chances are very good that many of your company's employees are posting personal content on the Internet. They may be posting at their own blog or website, or they may be posting at community sites and services—for example, uploading photos, adding comments to other websites, or exchanging parenting advice or recipes in a chat room. In some cases, however, employees may use these avenues for personal expression to vent about coworkers, supervisors, customers, and other workplace issues. And, some may express personal opinions—unrelated to their job—that could harm the company's reputation.

Employers face a dilemma. Most are understandably wary about trying to "crack down" on personal postings. After all, blogs and other personal sites are often a creative outlet, a way for friends and people with similar interests to stay in touch, a place to share opinions and be part of a larger community of Xena fans, pug owners, single parents, or recycling enthusiasts. They are, in a word, personal, and few employers really want to snoop through their employees' personal writings or be known as the company that stifles personal expression.

Unfortunately, however, not all employees like their jobs. An employee blog or other posted content that reveals company trade secrets, slams a company product that's about to be released, or threatens or harasses other employees can also be an unmitigated disaster for the company. Even posts that have nothing to do with work can create major workplace problems, if they express extreme and unpopular views, racist comments, or violent fantasies, for example. This chapter explains what you can and can't do in regulating employee posts, and provides policy language that gives employees some ground rules for Internet content.

## Entering the Blogosphere

According to a 2006 report by the Pew Internet & American Life Project, 12 million American adults keep blogs, and 57 million American adults read them. The majority of adults who keep a personal blog are young: 18 to 29 years old. Bloggers are more likely to be male than female. And, although most bloggers are white, the statistics for blogs aren't as skewed as for Internet use in general. While 75% of all Internet users in the United States are white, only 60% of bloggers are in that category. Almost 20% of bloggers classify themselves as Hispanic.

What do bloggers write about? Pretty much everything. There are blogs documenting the authors' dreams, diets, political views, health, pets, children, poetry, addictions, favorite TV shows, and more. Most bloggers say that a personal experience has inspired them to post to their blog. And, judging from the confessions to embarrassing, inappropriate, and sometimes illegal behavior (at times, accompanied by photographic evidence), it shouldn't be a surprise that more than half blog under a pseudonym.

Popular blog topics include:

- The bloggers' life/experiences    37%
- Politics and government:          11%
- Entertainment                      7%
- Sports                             6%
- News and current events            5%
- Technology                         4%
- Religion, spirituality, or faith   2%
- A specific hobby                   1%
- A health problem or illness        1%

Blogs aren't the only way to express opinions online. Internet users can create their own websites or Web pages; put photos, videos, music, or other artwork online; add comments to someone else's website or blog, or use micro-blogging sites such as Twitter.com. Pew estimates that 48 million American adults post content online, including 20 million who have their own webpage or website.

# Restrictions on Personal Posting

As an employer, you have the right to control what employees do with the time and equipment you pay for, generally speaking. When employees use their own computers to express their own opinions on their own time, however, an employer's legal rights are more limited—as is an employer's practical ability to crack down on employee blogging, not to mention an employer's incentive to take action that will undoubtedly alienate large numbers of employees.

In this situation, the best offense is a good defense. Your company can manage the potential legal exposure and bad publicity that could result from employee posts that cross the line—without going overboard in policing employee expression—by adopting a policy that lets employees know where the line is. This section explains some legal rules and practical considerations to keep in mind as you review your options.

 CAUTION

**If access to an employee site is restricted, an employer may face legal liability for accessing it.** When an employee posts to the Internet, that content is usually available for the world—and the employer—to see. However, if an employee restricts access to a blog or website, an employer who breaks into the site can get into trouble. That's what happened when the vice president of Hawaiian Airlines used an employee's name and password to access a private website created by a Hawaiian pilot, where the pilot and other authorized visitors (mainly other pilots and Hawaiian employees) posted bulletins critical of the airline, its officers, and the pilots' union. In this situation, the 9th Circuit Court of Appeals allowed the site's owner to go forward with his lawsuit against Hawaiian for violating the Stored Communications Act. (*Konop v. Hawaiian Airlines*, 302 F.3d 868 (9th Cir. 2002).)

## Legal Protections for Employees Who Post Online

Not surprisingly, there are a host of laws that protect an employee's right to speak freely online. Here's a rundown:

- **Off-duty conduct laws.** A number of states have passed laws that prohibit employers from disciplining or firing employees for activities they pursue off-site, on their own time. Although some of these laws were originally intended to protect smokers from discrimination—they tend to include language protecting employees who "use legal products" while off duty—others protect any employee conduct that doesn't break the law. These laws could provide legal protection for an employee who keeps a blog.

- **Protections for political views.** A handful of states protect employees from discrimination based on their political views or affiliation. In these states, disciplining an employee for personal posts that endorse a particular candidate or cause could be illegal.

- **Protections for "whistlebloggers."** An employee who raises concerns about safety hazards or illegal activity at work may be protected as a whistleblower (or a "whistleblogger," if the concerns are raised in a blog). Whistleblower protections recognize that the public good is served by employees who are willing to come forward with these types of complaints—and that very few employees will do so if they can be fired for it.

- **Prohibitions on retaliation.** A variety of employment laws protect employees from retaliation for claiming that their rights have been violated. If an employee's blog post complains of workplace discrimination, harassment, violation of the Family and Medical Leave Act, wage and hour violations, or other legal transgressions, that employee may be protected from disciplinary action.

- **Concerted activity protections.** The National Labor Relations Act and similar state laws protect employees' rights to communicate with each other about the terms and conditions of employment, and to join together, in a union or otherwise, to bring concerns about such issues to their employer. Under these laws, an employee who is fired for blogging about low wages, poor benefits, or long work hours, for example, could have a plausible legal claim.

**TIP**

**The First Amendment doesn't apply in private employment.** Many employees mistakenly believe that the right to free speech and freedom of the press, enshrined in the First Amendment of the U.S. Constitution, protects their right to say or write whatever they want online, in a blog or otherwise. However, the Constitution only protects individual rights as against government intrusion, not against private companies. If a state government tried to ban what private citizens could say on their blogs, that would raise a First Amendment issue. If the government isn't involved, however, the First Amendment doesn't come into play.

## Lessons From the Real World

**Employee fired for blogging wins wrongful termination case. In France.**

Catherine Sanderson, who blogs under the name Petite Anglaise, was fired from her job as a secretary for an English accounting firm doing business in Paris. She never named the firm, nor did she write much about her job at all. Her intent in starting a blog was to give "a Brit's eye view of Parisian life." She says that her occasional references to her job in the blog were "usually in the form of some embarrassing incident which had befallen me at work . . . invariably embellished a little, in order to increase their comedic value." She didn't identify the firm or herself in the blog, and used pseudonyms for those in her personal life whom she wrote about.

Her anonymity ended when she posted a couple of photographs of herself, however. She was fired in April of 2006 because of her blog. Although she was initially accused of "gross misconduct," the firm's lawyer later argued that she had risked damaging the company's reputation by blogging about it, that she had wasted company resources by blogging from work, and that she may have lied about her whereabouts on two half-days when her blog implied that she was meeting a lover in a hotel. If you're wondering why the firm had to have a lawyer argue its side, it's because Sanderson filed a wrongful dismissal case with the Paris Industrial Tribunal.

And she won, to the tune of one year's back pay and some reimbursement for her legal fees. The firm also had to reimburse the unemployment department for the six months when she collected benefits after being fired. As a result of publicity following the incident, Sanderson signed a book publishing deal reportedly worth half a million pounds. *Petite Anglaise* (subtitle: *In Paris. In Love. In Trouble*) was published in June 1008 in the United Stated.

## Practical Concerns When Limiting Personal Posts

In addition to legal concerns, there are also practical reasons why your company should tread carefully when seeking to regulate personal blogs and online posts.

- **The "POS" factor.** Children on the Internet often use the acronym POS (for "parent over shoulder") to indicate that they can't speak freely because a parent has entered the room. Employees are very likely to see your company restrictions on personal posting at home in the same way—overly restrictive and unnecessarily intrusive. Why should an employer care whether employees blog about their kitchen remodel, their children's health problems, or their favorite band? The more a company tries to limit what its employees do off duty, the more employees are likely to feel like prisoners or children, rather than valued members of a team.

- **Public relations concerns.** An employer that tries to prohibit or greatly restrict personal posting also runs into a potential public relations problem: The online community, particularly the "blogging community," doesn't like—and will publicize— efforts to silence one of their ranks. If an employee is fired for blogging, or even if a well-known company adopts an anti-blogging stance, other bloggers may be inspired to write about it, particularly if the company accused of wrongdoing has cultivated a beneficent public relations image. The result could be a "blog swarm" of bad PR for your company.

 **Lessons From the Real World**

**Lockheed employee blows the whistle on YouTube.**

Michael De Kort, an engineer at Lockheed Martin, was concerned about design flaws in work the company was doing to refurbish patrol boats for the Coast Guard. The flaws included blind spots in the boats' surveillance systems, security problems with the communications systems, and possible equipment malfunction in cold weather.

De Kort spoke to his supervisors, government investigators, and even members of Congress. He felt his concerns weren't being taken seriously, so he posted a video of himself talking about them on YouTube. Six months later, a government report confirmed some of his complaints. And, in January 2008, he received an award from the Society of Social Implications of Technology, for "high ethical standards in protecting or promoting the interests and safety of the public." Lockheed apparently didn't share the love for De Kort: He was fired shortly after posting the video, for what Lockheed said were cost-cutting reasons.

- **Enforcement problems.** It can be tough to enforce a restrictive policy on employee blogs. If they blog from home, how will you find out about it? Are you really going to dedicate human resources to finding and reading employee blogs? If an employee uses a pseudonym (as most bloggers do) and doesn't name your company or other employees, how are you going to know about the blog? How much time and effort is your company willing to put into policing employees' personal blogs? For most companies, the answer is not much (if any).

## Adopting a Commonsense Policy

Online postings are easy to dash off and virtually impossible to retract once published. When employees aren't at work, they probably aren't thinking of the potential consequences of making fun of a coworker's accent or revealing little-known facts about a client. Most likely, they're simply trying to be funny and attract readers.

What can your company do to curb inappropriate employee posts without going overboard? Adopt a policy letting employees know that their personal blogs could get them in trouble at work, and explain what types of content could be problematic.

### Blogs About Work: More Positive Than You Might Think

Most employers fear an employee blog or post that slams a company product, makes fun of coworkers, or otherwise shows the company in a bad light. Believe it or not, however, some research shows that employees who blog about work are fairly positive about their jobs. In the first six months of 2005, Edelman and Intelliseek tracked blogs for mentions of "love my job," "hate work," and "hate my boss," and found that "love my job" came up twice as often as "hate work," and four times as often as "hate my boss." You can find more results at Edelman's website, www.edelman.com; select "Insights," then "Talking From the Inside Out: The Rise of Employee Bloggers" (2005).

Having a written policy on personal posts puts employees on notice that their personal writings could get them into professional trouble (something that many employees seem not to fully understand). In short, it may remind them to think before they publish anything that may relate to the company.

To start your company's policy, you'll want to assure employees that the company supports their personal creative efforts, while also reminding them that discussing work on a personal blog can lead to problems.

---

**Personal Blogs and Online Posts**

Our Company recognizes that some of our employees may choose to express themselves by posting personal information on the Internet through personal websites, blogs, or chat rooms, by uploading content, or by making comments at other websites or blogs. We value our employees' creativity and honor your interest in engaging in these forms of personal expression on your own time, should you choose to do so.

However, problems can arise when a personal posting identifies or appears to be associated with our Company, or when a personal posting is used in ways that violate the Company's rights or the rights of other employees.

---

## No Posting Using Company Resources

Your policy should prohibit employees from using the company's computer systems to write or publish personal blog posts. While you might think few employees would blog from work, you'd be wrong: According to the Pew Project's 2006 report, 7% of bloggers "usually" blog from work, and another 6% blog from both home and work. Although these aren't the highest percentages, they're out of those 12 million who keep blogs—which means roughly a million and a half people blog at least some of the time from work.

---

**No Posting Using Company Resources**

You may not use Company resources to create or maintain a personal blog or a personal website, or to upload content or make personal postings online, nor may you do so on Company time.

---

## Ground Rules for Posting Content

Your company's policy should give employees some guidelines for posting online, whether to personal blogs, personal websites, or community sites. Your goal here is to make sure employees know that they blog at their own risk. Many employees don't realize that they can get into personal legal trouble for what they post. Despite a handful of well-publicized firings based on employee posts, some employees still don't realize that blogging about work can lead to the unemployment line.

By making sure employees know the risks, and setting down some ground rules for posts that deal with your company, your policy can encourage employees to stop and think before they hit "publish."

## Fired for Online Posting

Are you wondering how far an employee has to go to get fired for posting information or opinions on the Internet? Of course, it all depends on your company's philosophy, the employee's disciplinary history, how much damage the employee's post actually causes, and many other factors. Here are some real-world examples of posts that have led to termination, along with links to the blogs or news coverage of them:

- Microsoft fired temp employee Michael Hansom for posting photos of Macintosh computers arriving at Microsoft, with the tag line: "Even Microsoft wants G5s" (www.michaelhanscom. com/eclecticism/2003/10/23/even-microsoft-wants-g5s).

- Heather Armstrong was fired by her employer (whom she never identified on her blog) for humorous posts about annoying habits of her coworkers and company management, what she actually did when she was supposed to be working at home, among other things. Her website, www.dooce.com, brought the word "dooced" to the modern lexicon (it means to get fired for blogging).

- "Troutgirl," an engineer, was fired by Friendster for blogging about the company; she identified a couple of posts, including one about an overhaul of the company's site architecture, as the reasons for her termination (http://troutgirl.wordpress. com/2004/08).

- Jessica Zenner was fired by Nintendo based on unkind comments about coworkers and her job in her blog (www. thestranger.com/seattle/Content?oid=322407).

- Matt Donegan, a reporter and editor, was fired by *The Dover Post* after his MySpace blog, included an entry that complained about his African-American neighbors partying late into the night and speculated whether similar circumstances might have led to the assassination of Martin Luther King, Jr. Donegan said the post was intended as a joke. His employer was not LOL (www.nbc10.com/news/6667658/detail.html).

### Fired for Online Posting (continued)

- 27 employees were fired by the Automobile Club of Southern California for postings on MySpace about coworkers' sexual orientation and weight. The employees—some of whom used their own names in their posts—also had an online discussion of their plan to slow down the company's roadside assistance to motorists (www.msnbc.msn.com/id/8845731).

### Guidelines for Online Posting

You are legally responsible for content you post to the Internet, in a blog or otherwise. You can be held personally liable for defaming others, revealing trade secrets or proprietary information, and copyright infringement, among other things.

All of our Company policies apply to anything you write in a personal blog, post to the Internet, or upload to the Internet. This means, for example, that you may not use personal postings to harass or threaten other employees or reveal Company trade secrets or confidential information. Embarrassing or unkind comments about other Company employees, customers, clients, or competitors are also inappropriate.

If, in the process of making a personal post or upload on the Internet, you identify yourself as an employee of our Company, whether by explicit statement or by implication, you must clearly state that the views expressed in your post, or at your blog or website, are your own, and do not reflect the views of the Company.

You may not use Company trademarks, logos, or other images, nor may you make false or misleading statements about the Company's philosophy, products, services, opinions, or affiliations with other companies.

> The Company may have a legal duty not to disclose certain facts, such as information on stock offerings. Revealing this information on the Internet could cause very serious problems. If you have any concerns about the confidentiality or propriety of something you would like to post, check with your manager first.
>
> Please keep in mind that your personal postings will be read not only by your friends and family, but possibly by your coworkers and bosses, as well as our Company's customers, clients, and competitors. Even if you post anonymously or under a pseudonym, your identity can be discovered relatively easily. Use your common sense when deciding what to include in a post or comment. Don't say something that you wouldn't want these people to read.

**CAUTION**

**Don't forget the acknowledgment form.** If your company adopts the personal blogs and online posting policy covered in this chapter, make sure you require employees to sign an acknowledgment form. You'll find a sample acknowledgment form and instructions in Appendix B; a blank acknowledgment form is included on the CD-ROM at the back of this book.

# Putting It All Together: A Sample Blog and Personal Post Policy

Here's a sample blog and personal post policy adopted by a company that designs software. The company encourages employee creativity and independent thinking, so it doesn't want to be seen as banning employee's personal expression. Many of its employees keep their own blogs and post to a variety of online forums, however, so the company decides that it needs to establish guidelines.

## Personal Blogs and Online Posts

Our Company recognizes that some of our employees may choose to express themselves by posting personal information on the Internet through personal websites, blogs, or chat rooms, by uploading content, or by making comments at other websites or blogs. We value our employees' creativity and honor your interest in engaging in these forms of personal expression on your own time, should you choose to do so.

However, problems can arise when a personal posting identifies or appears to be associated with our Company, or when a personal posting is used in ways that violate the Company's rights or the rights of other employees.

### No Posting Using Company Resources

You may not use Company resources to create or maintain a personal blog or a personal website, or to upload content or make personal postings online, nor may you do so on Company time.

### Guidelines for Online Posting

You are legally responsible for content you post to the Internet, in a blog or otherwise. You can be held personally liable for defaming others, revealing trade secrets or proprietary information, and copyright infringement, among other things.

All of our Company policies apply to anything you write in a personal blog, post to the Internet, or upload to the Internet. This means, for example, that you may not use personal postings to harass or threaten other employees or reveal Company trade secrets or confidential information. Embarrassing or unkind comments about other Company employees, customers, clients, or competitors are also inappropriate.

If, in the process of making a personal post or upload on the Internet, you identify yourself as an employee of our Company, whether by explicit statement or by implication, you must clearly state that the views expressed in your post, or at your blog or website, are your own, and do not reflect the views of the Company.

You may not use Company trademarks, logos, or other images, nor may you make false or misleading statements about the Company's philosophy, products, services, opinions, or affiliations with other companies.

The Company may have a legal duty not to disclose certain facts, such as information on stock offerings. Revealing this information on the Internet could cause very serious problems. If you have any concerns about the confidentiality or propriety of something you would like to post, check with your manager first.

Please keep in mind that your personal postings will be read not only by your friends and family, but possibly by your coworkers and bosses, as well as our Company's customers, clients, and competitors. Even if you post anonymously or under a pseudonym, your identity can be discovered relatively easily. Use your common sense when deciding what to include in a post or comment. Don't say something that you wouldn't want these people to read.

# Cell Phones

## In This Chapter:

### Policy Provisions for Cell Phones

☐ Security of Company-Issued Cell Phones

☐ Personal Cell Phones at Work

☐ Don't Use a Cell Phone While Driving

    ☐ Optional Policy Language for Hands-Free Equipment

☐ Using Your Cell Phone for Business

Cell phones have changed the landscape of everyday life so much that it's hard to remember a time when they weren't everywhere. But that time wasn't so long ago. Cell phones didn't become a common consumer purchase until the 1990s or so, and even then few people used them as a primary means of communication. Today, however, the cell phone is a necessity of modern life. By June 2008, 84% of Americans had cell phones, according to research by CTIA-The Wireless Association. (You can find more statistics on cell phones at www.ctia.org; select "U.S. Wireless Quick Facts and Figures.")

## The First Call on a Portable Cell Phone

There was a lot going on in April 1973: France and the Netherlands recognized North Vietnam as a separate country; John Lennon and Yoko Ono formed their own country called Nutopia (its national anthem was silence, possibly preferable to the chart-topping single of the month, "Tie a Yellow Ribbon Round the Old Oak Tree," by Tony Orlando and Dawn); Richard Nixon announced the resignation of many of his top aides in the Watergate scandal; and Roberto Clemente's number was retired by the Pittsburgh Pirates. Oh, and Martin Cooper made the first public telephone call on a portable cell phone.

Of course, "portable" is in the eye of the beholder: The phone Cooper used weighed two and a half pounds and was ten inches long, and its battery died after 20 minutes. It was called "The Boot" because of its shape. At the time, Cooper worked for Motorola. He used his first phone call to contact a friend who worked at a rival company, AT&T's Bell Labs.

Unfortunately, the convenience of the cell phone can also be its curse—especially in the workplace. Cell phones can be distracting and disruptive at work, whether used in a shared workspace, during a business meeting, or while the owner should be helping customers or clients. They can even be dangerous—for example when used to transfer trade secrets, to eavesdrop in the company lunch room, or while driving. This chapter provides some policy language you can use to prevent common cell phone problems.

 **CROSS REFERENCE**
**This chapter covers only the "phone" feature of cell phones.**
Other chapters cover technologies that might be included with a cell phone, such as cameras (Chapter 9), instant messaging (Chapter 5), email (Chapter 3), and personal digital assistants (Chapter 8).

# Company-Owned Phones

If your company is one of the many that issue cell phones to employees, you'll need policy language covering a few issues: company ownership of the phones, personal calls, and theft prevention.

## Company Ownership of Phones

Your policy should start by telling employees that company-issued cell phones are company property, which employees must return upon request. This gives your company the ability to control the features on its cell phones (for example, to make sure that the employee's contact list can be erased remotely if the cell phone is stolen). It also establishes the company's right to inspect cell phones, if necessary, which in turn diminishes employees' expectations of privacy in company-issued cell phones.

> **Company-Issued Cell Phones**
>
> The Company may issue cell phones to employees whose jobs require them to make calls while away from work or require them to be accessible for work-related matters.
>
> Cell phones issued by the Company are Company property. Employees must comply with Company requests to make their Company-issued cell phones available for any reason, including upgrades, replacement, or inspection. Employees who leave the Company for any reason must turn in their Company-issued cell phones.

## Personal Use of Company Cell Phones

For a variety of reasons, the simplest policy is not to allow personal calls on company cell phones. Employees and managers won't have to review cell phone bills every month looking for numbers that aren't related to business. The company won't have to make judgment calls about how much personal use of a cell phone is too much. And calls made by customers, clients, and coworkers won't go straight to voicemail because an employee is too busy chatting with friends and family to pick up a work-related call.

Despite all the good reasons not to allow personal calls, however, an outright ban is impractical. Even the most conscientious employee may occasionally have to take a brief personal call. And allowing these calls—often, from a child, spouse, or partner who needs to check in—may help employees be more productive by alleviating pressing personal concerns. The policy below reflects those considerations.

**Personal Use of Company-Issued Cell Phones**

Company-issued cell phones are to be used only for business purposes. Although occasional, brief personal phone calls using a Company-issued phone are permitted, personal use that exceeds this standard will result in discipline, up to and including termination. Employees are expected to reimburse the Company for any costs or charges relating to personal use of their cell phones.

## Security of Company-Issued Phones

Employees may have phones full of text messages and client contact information, and they need to know how to keep it private. Your policy should also explain what employees should do if their company-issued phones are stolen.

**Security of Company-Issued Phones**

Employees are responsible for the security of Company-issued cell phones and the information stored on them. Always keep your cell phone with you when traveling; never leave it unattended in your car or hotel room. If your Company-issued cell phone is lost or stolen, notify the IT department immediately. Never store confidential Company information on a cell phone.

When using a cell phone, remember that your conversations are not necessarily private. Those around you can hear your end of the conversation. To protect the confidentiality of Company information (and avoid annoying others), please make cell phone calls in a private place.

---

**Personal Use of Company-Issued Cell Phones**

Cell phone transmissions may be intercepted. For this reason, employees should not conduct highly sensitive or confidential conversations by cell phone. If you have any questions about what types of conversations are appropriate for a cell phone and which are not, please ask your manager.

---

# Personal Cell Phones at Work

Most of your employees probably have personal cell phones that they bring to work. Apparently the main thing employees do with their personal cell phones—based on surveys—is annoy each other. These workplace annoyances result from loud ring tones, inappropriate personal conversations, interruptions to meetings and presentations, and rudeness to coworkers or customers while talking on the phone.

Some companies respond to these concerns by simply banning personal cell phones at work. For most employers, however, an outright ban is overkill. Allowing personal cell phones gives employees a chance to touch base with family members and friends while on breaks or at lunch, or to receive emergency messages during the day, all without using company phones. You can probably achieve the results you want—fewer interruptions and less time wasted—while allowing employees to have their cell phones at work by simply prohibiting employees from using cell phones (or allowing them to ring) at certain times, in particular locations, or for excessive amounts of time.

The policy language below contains basic cell phone etiquette for the workplace that most companies will want to adopt.

**Personal Cell Phones at Work**

Although our Company allows employees to bring their personal cell phones to work, we expect employees to keep personal conversations to a minimum. While occasional, brief personal phone calls are acceptable, frequent or lengthy personal calls can affect productivity and disturb others. For this reason, we generally expect employees to make and receive personal phone calls during breaks only.

Employees must turn off the ringers on their cell phones while away from their cell phones. If you share workspace with others, you must turn off the ringer on your phone while at work.

Employees must turn off their cell phones or leave their phones elsewhere while in meetings, presentations, or trainings. Employees must also turn off their cell phones or leave their phones elsewhere while meeting with clients or serving customers.

It is inappropriate to interrupt a face-to-face conversation with a coworker in order to take a personal phone call.

Remember, others can hear your cell phone conversations. Try to talk quietly, and save intimate discussions for another time.

Employees who violate this policy will be subject to discipline, up to and including termination.

### Annoying Ringtones: One of the Top Workplace Peeves

Since employees started bringing their cell phones to work, they've been annoying their coworkers with loud ringtones. According to a recent study by Randstad USA, employees find loud noises, including cell phone ring tones, to be one of the seven biggest pet peeves. Gossip, poor time management by coworkers, messiness in communal spaces (the Company kitchen or break room, for instance), potent scents, misuse of email, and overuse of personal communication devices—such as PDAs and cell phones—during meetings round out the list.

# Safety

Studies show that drivers who are distracted cause more accidents, and that cell phones and other forms of wireless technology are increasingly to blame for our lack of attention to the road—81% of drivers admit to talking on cell phones while driving, according to a 2008 survey by Nationwide Insurance Company. (You can find more results from the survey at www.nationwide.com; search for "DWD" (driving while distracted).)

### One Year, 100 Cars, 241 Drivers, and 82 Crashes

To get a better idea of why people get into car accidents, the National Highway Transportation Safety Association and the Virginia Tech Transportation Institute created an experiment: They put video and sensor equipment in 100 cars and tracked driver behavior for a year. And an eventful year it was, with more than two million miles driven, 82 crashes, 761 near-crashes, and more than 8,000 "critical incidents" (situations when the driver either got too close to another car, pedestrian, cyclist, animal, or object, or had to engage in crash

## One Year, 100 Cars, 241 Drivers, and
## 82 Crashes (continued)

avoidance behavior—swerving, braking, and so on—to stay out of trouble).

The study revealed that almost 80% of crashes involved some form of driver distraction or drowsiness, and the number one source of driver distraction was using a cell phone. A few more interesting facts:

- **Dialing is dangerous but ...** Although dialing a cell phone is significantly more dangerous than simply talking or listening on the phone, the number of accidents and near-accidents attributable to each activity was about the same because drivers spend so much more time talking and listening on the phone than dialing it.

- **Don't let a bug in the car—or try to swat it once it's there.** Reaching for a moving object makes a driver nine times more likely to get in an accident. Reading, applying makeup, and dialing a cell phone each increase the risk of an accident by a factor of three, but having an insect in the car increased the risk by a factor of seven.

- **Experience counts.** Drivers with more years of experience had far fewer crashes and near-crashes than relatively inexperienced drivers.

- **Better drivers just seem nicer.** Better drivers—those with fewer crashes and near-crashes—scored higher on tests that measured extroversion, openness to experience, agreeableness, and conscientiousness.

- **Don't hire this guy.** A relatively small number of drivers caused most of the problems. 27 of the drivers in the test were responsible for almost 75% of the crashes and near-crashes; one of them had 15 incidents in one year.

Want to know more? You can find all of the results, along with lots of graphs and even photos of the tracking devices in the cars, at the National Highway Traffic Safety Administration website (www.nhtsa.dot.gov). Click "Traffic Safety" on the navigation bar, then click "Drowsy and Distracted Driving" on the left side of the page.

To address these concerns, a growing number of states have passed laws that limit the use of cell phones while driving. These laws take several forms: Some require drivers to use a hands-free device if they want to talk on the phone, some prohibit younger or less experienced drivers from using any type of cell phone, and some allow officers to cite drivers for using a hand-held cell phone if the driver is pulled over for another offense.

### TIP

**Keep up on the laws of your state.** For detailed information on state driving safety laws, check out the website of the Governors Highway Safety Association at www.statehighwaysafety.org. Select "State Info and Laws" to see state law charts on a number of topics, including use of cell phones. The site, which is updated frequently, also has a number of other resources, including research and reports on various driver safety issues. Note that some local governments have also enacted cell phone restrictions, so check with your town, city, or county as well.

If your company does business in a state that limits the use of cell phones while driving, of course you'll want to require employees to follow the law. However, even companies in states that haven't legislated in this area need a cell phone policy. Simply put, using a cell phone while driving is dangerous. And, if an employee causes an accident while doing business on a cell phone, your company could be held liable for the damages.

## Cell Phones + Driving Employees = Company Liability

There have been plenty of big settlements in lawsuits against companies whose employees injured or killed someone while talking on a cell phone. Why are the companies sued? Because they typically have much deeper pockets that the employee who actually caused the accident. Consider these examples:

- A stockbroker from Smith Barney was making a cold call to a potential client while driving when he struck and killed a motorcyclist. Although the broker was using his own cell phone and driving to a nonbusiness event, the plaintiff argued that Smith Barney should be found liable because it encouraged employees to use their cell phones for cold calling without training them on safety issues. Smith Barney eventually settled the case for $500,000.

- A lawyer was making a business call on her cell phone while driving home from work. She hit something, which she thought was a deer, and kept driving; sadly, she actually hit—and killed—a teenager. The attorney served a year in jail for hit-and-run driving and was ordered to pay the victim's family more than $2 million; her law firm settled its part of the case for an undisclosed amount.

- An employee of International Paper was using her company cell phone when she rear-ended another driver on the freeway, causing injuries that eventually required the other driver to have her arm amputated. The company paid $5.2 million to settle the case.

It really doesn't matter whether your company issues cell phones to employees or not: If your company's employees do business by phone, your company needs a cell phone policy. Not only will this help protect the safety of company employees and those they might encounter on the road, but it will also help your company avoid liability for accidents.

**Don't Use a Cell Phone While Driving**

We know that our employees may use their cell phones for work-related matters, whether these devices belong to the employee or are issued by the Company.

Employees are prohibited from using cell phones for work-related matters while driving. We are concerned for your safety and for the safety of other drivers and pedestrians, and using a cell phone while driving can lead to accidents.

If you must make a work-related call while driving, you must wait until you can pull over safely and stop the car before placing your call. If you receive a work-related call while driving, you must ask the caller to wait while you pull over safely and stop the car. If you are unable to pull over safely, you must tell the caller that you will have to call back when it is safe to do so.

If your company wants to allow employees to use a hands-free device to talk on the phone while driving, you can add the language below to the end of the policy. If your company issues cell phones to employees for work-related calls, it should also issue them hands-free equipment to allow them to use the phones in accordance with this part of the policy. Keep in mind, however, that some studies have shown that the use of hands-free equipment does not significantly eliminate the risk of accidents from talking on a cell phone.

Currently, no state prohibits adult, experienced drivers from using hands-free devices while driving, except for certain professions (such as school bus drivers). Before you adopt the policy language below, check on the laws of your state and local government to make sure that hands-free devices are still allowed.

**Hands-Free Equipment**

Employees may use hands-free equipment to make or answer calls while driving without violating this policy. However, safety must always be your first priority. We expect you to keep these calls brief. If, because of weather, traffic conditions, or any other reason, you are unable to concentrate fully on the road, you must either end the conversation or pull over and safely park your vehicle before resuming your call.

# Wage and Hour Concerns

As portable technology improves, it's becoming easier for employees to work anywhere, at almost any time. The benefits of this trend are obvious: higher productivity, opportunities for telecommuting, improved work-life balance for employees, even reducing greenhouse gases as fewer employees have to commute each day.

There's a significant legal downside to consider, however. When nonexempt employees—those who are entitled to earn overtime—work away from their usual worksite, those hours might not get recorded, and the employee may not receive overtime pay, in violation of wage and hour laws.

The Fair Labor Standards Act (FLSA) is the federal law that governs wages and hours. Among other things, the FLSA requires employers to pay nonexempt employees overtime if they work more than 40 hours in a week; some state laws have daily overtime standards. Employees must be paid for every hour the employer "suffers or permits" them to work. This rule has been interpreted fairly strictly against employers: If employees are working overtime hours, and your company knows or should know about it, the employees are entitled to overtime pay.

Cell phones create a problem because employees can use them anywhere at any time. Employees who make a few work-related calls on the weekend or after hours might be entitled to overtime. This is true whether they use their own phones or a phone issued by the company. And, it will be tough for the company to find out about these extra hours until it's too late: Often, a company only discovers that an employee thinks he or she should have earned overtime when it is served with a lawsuit or complaint from the federal or state labor department.

The best way to avoid these problems is to adopt a policy prohibiting employees from making unauthorized calls on their own time. The policy below also lets employees know that they shouldn't use their personal phones for work-related calls, to make record keeping easier.

---

**Using Your Cell Phone for Business**

Our Company's overtime rules apply to any type of work done after hours, including using a Company-issued cell phone to make business calls. All overtime work—including such work-related calls—must be approved in writing, in advance. Working overtime without permission violates Company policy and may result in disciplinary action.

Employees may not use their own personal cell phones to make business calls. If you feel that you need a cell phone to perform your job, please ask your manager to get you a Company-issued cell phone.

---

CAUTION

**If they work, you must pay.** Even if your company requires employees to get approval before working overtime, it should pay for the overtime hours they work—including hours that aren't authorized. Discipline employees who work unapproved overtime, but pay them for those hours. This is a much safer approach than having to argue later, to a labor commissioner or judge, that your company didn't "suffer or permit" the work.

CAUTION

**Don't forget the acknowledgment form.** If your company adopts the cell phone policy covered in this chapter, make sure you require employees to sign an acknowledgment form. You'll find a sample acknowledgment form and instructions in Appendix B; a blank acknowledgment form is included on the CD-ROM at the back of this book.

## Putting It All Together: Sample Cell Phone Policy

Here's a sample cell phone policy adopted by a company that sells and repairs office equipment. The company has issued cell phones to its sales and service staff, who make numerous work-related calls every day and are often away from the office. Because employees spend much of their day driving to and from client businesses, the company is also very concerned about driving safety—so much so that it decides not to allow hands-free devices.

# Cell Phone Policy

### Company-Issued Cell Phones

The Company may issue cell phones to employees whose jobs require them to make calls while away from work or require them to be accessible for work-related matters.

Cell phones issued by the Company are Company property. Employees must comply with Company requests to make their Company-issued cell phones available for any reason, including upgrades, replacement, or inspection. Employees who leave the Company for any reason must turn in their Company-issued cell phones.

### Personal Use of Company-Issued Cell Phones

Company-issued cell phones are to be used only for business purposes. Although occasional, brief personal phone calls using a Company-issued phone are permitted, personal use that exceeds this standard will result in discipline, up to and including termination. Employees are expected to reimburse the Company for any costs or charges relating to personal use of their cell phones.

### Security of Company-Issued Phones

Employees are responsible for the security of Company-issued cell phones and the information stored on them. Always keep your cell phone with you when traveling; never leave it unattended in your car or hotel room. If your Company-issued cell phone is lost or stolen, notify the IT department immediately. Never store confidential Company information on a cell phone.

When using a cell phone, remember that your conversations are not necessarily private. Those around you can hear your end of the conversation. To protect the confidentiality of Company information (and avoid annoying others), please make cell phone calls in a private place.

Cell phone transmissions may be intercepted. For this reason, employees should not conduct highly sensitive or confidential conversations by cell phone. If you have any questions about what types of conversations are appropriate for a cell phone and which are not, please ask your manager.

**Personal Cell Phones at Work**

Although our Company allows employees to bring their personal cell phones to work, we expect employees to keep personal conversations to a minimum. While occasional, brief personal phone calls are acceptable, frequent or lengthy personal calls can affect productivity and disturb others. For this reason, we generally expect employees to make and receive personal phone calls during breaks only.

Employees must turn off the ringers on their cell phones while away from their cell phones. If you share workspace with others, you must turn off the ringer on your phone while at work.

Employees must turn off their cell phones or leave their phones elsewhere while in meetings, presentations, or trainings. Employees must also turn off their cell phones or leave their phones elsewhere while meeting with clients or serving customers.

It is inappropriate to interrupt a face-to-face conversation with a coworker in order to take a personal phone call.

Remember, others can hear your cell phone conversations. Try to talk quietly, and save intimate discussions for another time.

Employees who violate this policy will be subject to discipline, up to and including termination.

### Don't Use a Cell Phone While Driving

We know that our employees may use their cell phones for work-related matters, whether these devices belong to the employee or are issued by the Company.

Employees are prohibited from using cell phones for work-related matters while driving. We are concerned for your safety and for the safety of other drivers and pedestrians, and using a cell phone while driving can lead to accidents.

If you must make a work-related call while driving, you must wait until you can pull over safely and stop the car before placing your call. If you receive a work-related call while driving, you must ask the caller to wait while you pull over safely and stop the car. If you are unable to pull over safely, you must tell the caller that you will have to call back when it is safe to do so.

### Using Your Cell Phone for Business

Our Company's overtime rules apply to any type of work done after hours, including using a Company-issued cell phone to make business calls. All overtime work—including such work-related calls—must be approved in writing, in advance. Working overtime without permission violates Company policy and may result in disciplinary action.

Employees may not use their own personal cell phones to make business calls. If you feel that you need a cell phone to perform your job, please ask your manager to get you a Company-issued cell phone.

# Portable Computing Devices: PDAs, Laptops, and Beyond

*In This Chapter:*

## Policy Provisions for Portable Computing Devices

☐ Personal Use of Portable Computing Devices

☐ Use of Portable Computing Devices Is Not Private

☐ Content Rules for Portable Computing Devices

☐ Security of Portable Computing Devices

☐ Don't Use Personal Portable Computing Devices for Work

☐ No Texting While Driving

☐ Overtime and Portable Computing Devices

As processing power grows and microchip size shrinks, the tech world is witnessing a convergence of portable computing devices. Handheld personal digital assistants (PDAs) like the BlackBerry are packed with more software and memory, while laptop computers are shrinking in size, with models in stores today weighing in at only two or three pounds. At the same time, certain personal computing products have become industry specific—for example, the Amazon Kindle and Sony Reader are used extensively by publishers, and GPS-enabled electronic clipboards are used by UPS and FedEx employees.

There is no single name for all of these portable computing devices, but whether you call them smartphones, laptops, handhelds, or PDAs, they have something in common: Employees use them to do their jobs remotely, at home, and on the road.

### BlackBerry Still Tastes Sweetest for Business

Which portable device do most companies buy and support for their employees? It's still the BlackBerry: According to a recent survey, almost ¾ of companies that provide their employees with handheld computers use some version of the BlackBerry. Palm products (remember when the term "Palm Pilot" was synonymous with the personal digital assistant?) are running a very distant second, with 18% of the market.

But there's an up and comer in the ranks: the iPhone, by Apple. Although the iPhone currently has only 5% of the business market, it got the highest ranking for user satisfaction. And a significant percentage of companies surveyed said they had plans to buy enterprise iPhones in the near future. In addition, surveys have shown that users of iPhones send and download significantly more data over their devices than users of competing devices.

Like the other technologies discussed in this book, however, portable computing devices bring increased risk with their increased efficiency. The most significant of these risks is from the theft or loss of company information. The very portability of these devices makes them a target for thieves—and all too easy to leave behind in a cab, restaurant, or hotel room. These devices may also expose the company's network to risks (if they can link into the company servers) and provide a backdoor for opportunistic hackers and viruses.

Because these devices are intended to allow employees to work away from the office, they can also create potentially huge liability for overtime work that the company doesn't know about or pay for. Finally, like cell phones, these devices can lead to safety problems and legal exposure for the company if employees use them while driving.

# Use Rules

Like other types of company-issued technology, portable computing devices can easily be put to personal use. Employees may use their company smartphones to call friends and family, their company laptops to send personal email and chat on the Internet, or their electronic readers to review their Great American Novel. Your company should make clear that its policies on appropriate use apply with equal force to portable computing devices. You should also cover personal use of company equipment. And, your policy must make clear that employees have no right to privacy in what they write or store on company-issued portable devices.

## Personal Use

There's no way around it: Employees are likely to use portable computing devices for personal reasons. That's why your company needs a policy on personal use of these devices. Like the policies in earlier chapters for email and the Internet, the policy language below allows limited personal use, but also warns employees that excessive use will led to discipline. It also requires employees to reimburse your company for more than occasional personal use.

---

**Personal Use of Company-Issued Portable Computing Devices**

The Company may provide you with a portable computing device (such as a laptop computer, smartphone, personal digital assistant, or [*if your company uses an industry-specific device, add it here*]). The Company may also permit you to access its network using a portable computing device to perform your job.

The Company's portable computing devices and network are intended for business use. You may use such computing devices for occasional personal purposes, but you may do so during nonwork hours only. You must also ensure that your personal use of portable computing devices does not interfere in any way with your job duties or performance. Any employee who abuses this privilege may be subject to discipline, up to and including termination.

If an employee's use of a Company-owned portable computing device results in fees or costs beyond what the Company would otherwise have to pay for the service, the employee will be required to reimburse the Company.

---

## Privacy

Your policy must also warn employees that they have no privacy in the information stored on portable computing devices. (See Chapters 1 and 3 for information about employee privacy and company-owned equipment.)

> ### Use of Portable Computing Devices Is Not Private
>
> The Company has the ability to access and review all information stored on the Company's portable computing devices and network. The Company reserves the right to perform such an inspection at any time, for any reason. You should not expect that any files, records, or other data stored on the Company's equipment and network will be private, even if you attempt to protect its privacy (for example, by using a password or designating it as "personal").

## Appropriate Content

You need not repeat all of the content rules for the various capabilities of portable computing devices (email, instant messaging, and Internet access, for example). Instead, you can refer back to those policies here, with a reminder that they apply to portable computing devices as well.

> ### Content Rules for Portable Computing Devices
>
> All of our policies and rules of conduct apply to employee use of Company-issued portable computing devices. All communications (email, instant messaging, and Internet access) on Company-issued portable computing devices are subject to the Company's policies on appropriate use. This means, for example, that employees may not send harassing messages, access pornographic or gambling websites, or violate any of the Company's other rules on appropriate communications content.

# Security

Because of their small size and portability, laptops, PDAs, and smartphones are easily lost or stolen. And, because they are often intended to allow employees to access the company's network remotely, these devices present virus and hacking threats, whether they remain in the employee's possession or fall into the wrong hands.

---

### Land of the Lost: PDAs and Laptops Often Missing in Action

If you're one of those people who never has to wonder where you left the car keys, you may find it hard to believe that people really lose their laptops and PDAs. But they do, in very large numbers, and often with sensitive information on them.

According to a 2004 survey of executives, more than one-third of their companies issued PDAs to at least some employees. More than 80% of them carry valuable or somewhat valuable information on those PDAs, and 38% use their PDAs to access corporate networks. Given those numbers, you'd hope they were carefully guarding that precious information—but you'd be wrong: Half of the respondents said they had no security features on their PDAS, and almost a quarter of them admit having a PDA lost or stolen. (2004 U.S. PDA Business Usage Survey: www.pdatoday.com/more/A1460_0_1.)

Laptops don't fare any better: A survey of IT professionals revealed that 81% of the companies they worked for had lost at least one laptop containing sensitive information in the past year. And, in 2005 alone, 750,000 laptops were stolen. (Elena Malykhina, "Laptop Lockdown Checklist: Six Technologies to Watch," *InformationWeek*, April 2, 2007.)

---

Employees need to know how to protect their portable devices and the data on them. Your policy should cover security issues such as encryption, theft prevention, and antivirus technology. Your policy should also cover whether and how employees may use their own portable computing devices for work, including accessing the company's network.

> ⚠ **CAUTION**
>
> **Don't forget your reporting obligations.** According to the National Conference of State Legislatures, 43 states and the District of Columbia have enacted notification statutes, which require companies to tell consumers if their personal information has been stolen or otherwise compromised. To find out what your state requires, go to the Conference's website, www.ncsl.org. Under the "Issue Areas" tab, select "Telecommunications & Information Technology," then "Privacy."

## Security Concerns for Company-Issued Devices

Use the policy below to tell employees how to secure the information on their company-issued portable computing devices.

---

**Security of Portable Computing Devices**

Although portable computing equipment (such as laptops, personal digital assistants, or smartphones) can greatly improve our communications and efficiency, they can also pose a risk to the security of the Company's proprietary information. If these devices are lost, stolen, or hacked into, an outsider could have access to Company data or the Company's network.

To prevent theft and loss of data, employees who receive Company-issued portable computing equipment must follow these guidelines:

Employees should not download confidential Company information to a portable computing device unless it is absolutely necessary. If confidential Company information is stored on a portable computing device, you must delete that information securely as soon as you are finished using it. If you are not certain whether particular data qualifies as confidential Company information, ask your supervisor for assistance.

All data and files kept on a portable computing device must be encrypted, using Company-approved encryption software.

All Company-issued portable computing devices will require power-on passwords, which must be changed every two months. You must always log or sign off before leaving a portable computing device unattended.

If your Company-issued portable computing device is equipped with antivirus software, you must download or install updates to this software when instructed by the Company.

You may not download, install, or use any software programs on a Company-issued portable computing device unless that program has been approved by the IT department.

Use the same malware precautions when using a portable computing device as are required for Company computers. Do not open attachments to email or instant messages if you do not know the sender or otherwise aren't sure that the attachment is legitimate. Do not open, read, or download any file from the Internet without scanning it for viruses.

Employees are responsible for the security of portable computing devices issued to them. Keep portable computing devices in your possession whenever possible. If you must leave a portable computing device unattended, you must store it out of sight in a secure location, such as a hotel safe or locked filing cabinet at home. Never leave a portable computing device in a vehicle.

Employees must immediately notify the Company's IT department if their portable computing device is lost or stolen, so the Company may remotely delete all data stored on the device.

## International Employers: Don't Let Trade Secrets Slip Out at the Border

The 9th Circuit Court of Appeals recently ruled that U.S. Customs and Border Patrol agents can search the contents of a traveler's laptop even if they don't have any particular reason to suspect wrongdoing. In *U.S. v. Arnold*, No. 06-50581 (April 21, 2008), the Court found no reason to exclude evidence of child pornography that Border Patrol agents found on Michael Arnold's laptop when he arrived at Los Angeles International Airport after a trip to the Philippines. Although the Fourth Amendment of the U.S. Constitution requires reasonable suspicion to search, border searches are presumed reasonable because of the government's strong interest in preventing unwanted people and items entering the country.

Let's hope that your company's employees never find themselves in exactly this situation. Even so, if your employees take laptops, PDAs, or handheld digital devices on a foreign business trip, they risk losing those devices—and the information on them—to Border Patrol agents, who sometimes confiscate such items. Your company's proprietary information and personal data about employees or customers, may be seized.

The Asian Law Caucus and the Electronic Frontier Foundation have filed a Freedom of Information Act lawsuit, seeking to require the Department of Homeland Security to hand over its policies and procedures regarding these searches and seizures, including how the Department safeguards confidential information taken from travelers. In the meantime, however, experts advise companies to limit the proprietary and personal information employees keep on their laptops and PDAs when crossing international borders.

## Security Concerns for Personal Portable Computing Devices

What happens when employees use their own devices for work instead of a company-issued device? Unfortunately, the controls discussed for company-issued equipment (restricting unauthorized access, choosing which employees receive a device, use of encryption, and the installation of software) may not exist for the employee's personal device. As long as your company can afford to issue portable computing devices to employees, the safest policy by far is to prohibit employees from using their own devices for work.

---

**Don't Use Personal Portable Computing Devices for Work**

We understand that employees may occasionally wish to use their own portable computing devices—such as laptops and smartphones—for work. However, storing Company information on a personal portable computing device or using such a device to access the Company's network creates unacceptable security risks. Therefore, employees are prohibited from using their own portable computing devices for business purposes or from storing Company information on a personal computing device. If you feel that you need a portable computing device to do your job, please talk to your manager to find out whether you are eligible for a Company-issued device.

---

## Lessons From the Real World

**Fall into the (liability) Gap: Stolen laptops compromise job applicant data.**

Joel Ruiz applied for a job at one of Gap's clothing stores in 2006. As part of the application process, Ruiz provided personal information, including his Social Security number. In 2007, Gap notified Ruiz and 800,000 other applicants that two of its laptops, which contained their application data in unencrypted form, had been stolen. Gap offered each applicant a year of free credit monitoring and fraud assistance, along with some identity theft insurance.

Ruiz filed a class action lawsuit against Gap, claiming that the company acted negligently, violated his privacy, and committed an unfair business practice, among other things. Gap argued that Ruiz's claims should be thrown out. There was no proof that Ruiz's information had been accessed or used in any way, so he couldn't show that he had suffered actual harm—an essential element of a lawsuit.

Although the court expressed skepticism—cautioning Ruiz that his suit might yet be thrown out, and that it was difficult to see how he could collect money damages—it found that Ruiz had alleged enough harm, including an increased risk of identity theft, to continue with his suit.

*Ruiz v. Gap, Inc.*, 540 F.Supp.2d 1121 (N.D. Cal. 2008).

# Driving Safety

Like cell phones, the use of PDAs and smartphones while driving can be very dangerous. In fact, texting while driving is more dangerous than talking on the phone, according to a study by the University of Utah: Those talking on a cell phone are four times more likely to get into an accident than people driving without distractions, while texting increases the likelihood of an accident by six times. The same study also shows that texting slows driver reaction times.

## No DWT in NJ and WA

One of the hottest issues in statehouses across the country these days is DWT: driving while texting. So far, a handful of states have banned it outright, and many more are considering legislation to prohibit drivers from using wireless communications devices while driving.

In some states, high-profile accidents may have helped push the legislation along. In Washington, for example, a driver was using his BlackBerry and failed to see that the traffic ahead of him on Interstate 5 had stopped; he crashed into a minivan, setting off a pileup that also involved four other cars and a bus. Several months later, the Washington legislature outlawed texting by drivers.

In New Jersey, the state legislature began considering its anti-texting law within a month after Governor Jon Corzine was badly injured in a car crash. Corzine, who was in the passenger seat, wasn't wearing his seat belt. What's more, his driver—who was doing 91 mph in a 65 zone—was investigated by state troopers who wanted to know whether he was texting (with his alleged girlfriend's husband) at the time of the accident.

A number of other states are considering similar laws. You can find out what your state is up to at the website of the National Conference on State Legislatures, www.ncsl.org; select "Traffic Safety" in the "Transportation" issue area. Is legislation really necessary to prevent something so obviously dangerous? Unfortunately, yes: 85% of respondents to one survey said they would not DWT if it were illegal.

Despite the somewhat obvious fact that texting while driving is dangerous, however, more than half of all drivers admit to doing it. In response, states are enacting and considering bans on texting while driving. And companies are adopting policies prohibiting employees from doing so, too. Just like using a cell phone, texting while driving can lead to accidents—and to liability for your company.

### No Texting While Driving

Employees are prohibited from using any portable computing device for work-related matters while driving. We are concerned for your safety and for the safety of other drivers and pedestrians, and texting, checking messages, going online, or otherwise using a portable computing device while driving can lead to accidents.

If you must send or read a work-related message while driving, you must wait until you can pull over safely and stop the car before doing so.

## Lessons From the Real World

**If you don't know where you're going, pull over.**

An employee of Berry Electric Contracting Company got lost while driving a company van in Arlington Heights, a Chicago suburb. He was trying to use the navigation device on his BlackBerry when he ran a red light and hit another car.

The driver of the other car, a 71-year-old woman, had to undergo five surgeries as a result of the crash. She lost some range of motion in her neck, has metal holding her pelvis together, and has permanent vision problems as a result of the crash. She sued the company. Right before trial, the case settled for $4.1 million, which was paid by Berry Electric's insurance carrier.

Abdon M. Pallasch, "$4 Mil. Award in BlackBerry Car Accident," *The Chicago Sun Times*, December 9, 2006.

# Wage and Hour Concerns

Personal computing devices make it possible for employees to work offsite, 24 x 7 x 365. This ability to work overtime can open your company up to significant legal exposure for wage and hour claims.

When nonexempt employees—those who are entitled to earn overtime—work away from their usual worksite, those hours might not get recorded, and the employee may not receive overtime pay, in violation of wage and hour laws. Employees who check their email after hours or work on documents from home might be entitled to overtime. And, the company might not know about these extra hours until it hears from a lawyer. (For more detailed information on overtime liability, see Chapter 7.)

The best way to control your company's liability is to adopt a policy requiring employees to get written authorization before using their handheld computers or other portable technology outside of their usual hours. The policy below also lets employees know that they shouldn't use their own laptops or handheld computers for work, to make record keeping easier.

---

**Overtime and Portable Computing Devices**

Our Company's overtime rules apply to any type of work done after hours, including using a Company-issued portable computing device (laptop, PDA, or smartphone, etc.) for work. All overtime work—including work done on a personal computing device—must be approved in writing, in advance. Working overtime without permission violates Company policy and may result in disciplinary action.

Employees may not use their own personal computing devices for work. If you feel that you need a personal computing device to perform your job, please talk to your manager to find out whether you are eligible for a Company-issued device.

---

## The PDA Lawsuits Are Coming!

You seldom find lawyers on opposite sides of the fence seeing eye to eye, but personal computing devices (particularly PDAs, like the BlackBerry and iPhone) have brought employment lawyers together. Whether they represent employees or employers, lawyers agree that portable computing devices will lead to lawsuits for unpaid overtime.

As reported in *The National Law Journal*, management lawyers are starting to advise clients to take steps to avoid these lawsuits, such as giving company-issued portable computing devices only to exempt employees (those who aren't eligible to earn overtime) and requiring employees to get permission before using them outside of their regular work hours.

What the two sides don't agree on is what's fueling the trend. Lawyers who advise employers claim that employee lawyers are "trolling" for these suits, actively looking for employees to serve as plaintiffs in class action lawsuits. Lawyers who represent employees counter that there's no need to manufacture a lawsuit where, as in this case, the law clearly favors the employee.

Whether or not some employee lawyers are trying to drum up this type of business, they're right about the law: Nonexempt employees are entitled to be paid for overtime the employer "suffers or permits." In the past, an employee who claimed to have done extra work at home or in some other offsite location often had a hard time both proving that the company knew or should have known about the hours, and coming up with some evidence of those hours. Portable computing devices like PDAs go a long way toward solving both of these proof problems for employees, because they show when documents and messages are accessed.

Tresa Baldas, "BlackBerry Clicks Can Up Company Costs," *The National Law Journal*, April 28, 2008.

> ⓘ **CAUTION**
>
> **Don't forget the acknowledgment form.** If your company adopts the portable computing device policy covered in this chapter, make sure you require employees to sign an acknowledgment form. You'll find a sample acknowledgment form and instructions in Appendix B; a blank acknowledgment form is included on the CD-ROM at the back of this book.

# Putting It All Together: Sample Portable Computing Device Policy

Here's a sample portable computing device policy adopted by a company that produces a variety of online content, including a daily subscription news service. Among its employees are reporters, programmers, developers, and so on, many of whom work from home and/or travel for work. Company employees have a number of company-issued portable computing devices, such as laptops and PDAs.

# Portable Computing Device Policy

## Personal Use of Company-Issued Portable Computing Devices

The Company may provide you with a portable computing device (such as a laptop computer, smartphone, personal digital assistant, or Kindle. The Company may also permit you to access its network using a portable computing device to perform your job.

The Company's portable computing devices and network are intended for business use. You may use such computing devices for occasional personal purposes, but you may do so during nonwork hours only. You must also ensure that your personal use of portable computing devices does not interfere in any way with your job duties or performance. Any employee who abuses this privilege may be subject to discipline, up to and including termination.

If an employee's use of a Company-owned portable computing device results in fees or costs beyond what the Company would otherwise have to pay for the service, the employee will be required to reimburse the Company.

## Use of Portable Computing Devices Is Not Private

The Company has the ability to access and review all information stored on the Company's portable computing devices and network. The Company reserves the right to perform such an inspection at any time, for any reason. You should not expect that any files, records, or other data stored on the Company's equipment and network will be private, even if you attempt to protect its privacy (for example, by using a password or designating it as "personal").

### Content Rules for Portable Computing Devices

All of our policies and rules of conduct apply to employee use of Company-issued portable computing devices. All communications (email, instant messaging, and Internet access) on Company-issued portable computing devices are subject to the Company's policies on appropriate use. This means, for example, that employees may not send harassing messages, access pornographic or gambling websites, or violate any of the Company's other rules on appropriate communications content.

### Security of Portable Computing Devices

Although portable computing equipment (such as laptops, personal digital assistants, or smartphones) can greatly improve our communications and efficiency, they can also pose a risk to the security of the Company's proprietary information. If these devices are lost, stolen, or hacked into, an outsider could have access to Company data or the Company's network.

To prevent theft and loss of data, employees who receive Company-issued portable computing equipment must follow these guidelines:

Employees should not download confidential Company information to a portable computing device unless it is absolutely necessary. If confidential Company information is stored on a portable computing device, you must delete that information securely as soon as you are finished using it. If you are not certain whether particular data qualifies as confidential Company information, ask your supervisor for assistance.

All data and files kept on a portable computing device must be encrypted, using Company-approved encryption software.

All Company-issued portable computing devices will require power-on passwords, which must be changed every two months.

You must always log or sign off before leaving a portable computing device unattended.

If your Company-issued portable computing device is equipped with antivirus software, you must download or install updates to this software when instructed by the Company.

You may not download, install, or use any software programs on a Company-issued portable computing device unless that program has been approved by the IT department.

Use the same malware precautions when using a portable computing device as are required for Company computers. Do not open attachments to email or instant messages if you do not know the sender or otherwise aren't sure that the attachment is legitimate. Do not open, read, or download any file from the Internet without scanning it for viruses.

Employees are responsible for the security of portable computing devices issued to them. Keep portable computing devices in your possession whenever possible. If you must leave a portable computing device unattended, you must store it out of sight in a secure location, such as a hotel safe or locked filing cabinet at home. Never leave a portable computing device in a vehicle.

Employees must immediately notify the Company's IT department if their portable computing device is lost or stolen, so the Company may remotely delete all data stored on the device.

### Don't Use Portable Computing Devices for Work

We understand that employees may occasionally wish to use their own portable computing devices—such as laptops and smartphones—for work. However, storing Company information on a personal portable computing device or using such a device to access the Company's network creates unacceptable security risks. Therefore, employees are prohibited from using their own portable computing devices for business purposes or from storing Company information on a personal computing device. If you feel that you need a portable computing device to do your job, please talk to your manager to find out whether you are eligible for a Company-issued device.

### No Texting While Driving

Employees are prohibited from using any portable computing device for work-related matters while driving. We are concerned for your safety and for the safety of other drivers and pedestrians, and texting, checking messages, going online, or otherwise using a portable computing device while driving can lead to accidents.

If you must send or read a work-related message while driving, you must wait until you can pull over safely and stop the car before doing so.

### Overtime and Portable Computing Devices

Our Company's overtime rules apply to any type of work done after hours, including using a Company-issued portable computing device (laptop, PDA, or smartphone, etc.) for work. All overtime work—including work done on a personal computing device—must be approved in writing, in advance. Working overtime without permission violates Company policy and may result in disciplinary action.

Employees may not use their own personal computing devices for work. If you feel that you need a personal computing device to perform your job, please talk to your manager to find out whether you are eligible for a Company-issued device.

# Cameras and Camera Phones

*In This Chapter:*

## Policy Provisions for Cameras and Camera Phones

☐ Alternative 1: Banning Camera Phones and Other Recording Devices

☐ Alternative 2: Use Restrictions

    ☐ Prohibiting Cameras in Certain Areas

    ☐ Prohibiting Use of Cameras

    ☐ Guidelines for Camera Use

P hones are not the only digital devices that incorporate cameras: You can also find cameras on PDAs (personal digital assistants), MP3 players, and even binoculars. But camera phones are certainly the most prevalent and, as a result, have brought us many images we might never have seen otherwise, captured by people who just happened to have their phones with them. These images have exposed scandals, captured natural disasters, and caught celebrities in compromising positions. They've given rise to the "citizen journalist," ready to provide evidence of breaking events as they happen.

## You Can Thank the Camera Phone

Don't believe that camera phones have already had a major impact on the way we see the world? Consider these images, all captured on camera phone:

- the execution of Saddam Hussein
- the London tube bombing
- protests in Myanmar by Buddhist monks
- the Asian tsunami
- the shootings at Virginia Tech, and
- some of the images of prisoner abuse from Abu Ghraib.

Of course, not all of the famous photos taken with camera phones are this weighty. You can also toss into the pile a picture of French soccer star Zinedine Zidane smoking a cigarette, after having starred in an antismoking campaign; pictures of Prince Harry dressed as a Nazi for a costume party; and the video of Michael Richards (who played Kramer on "Seinfeld") going off on a racist rant in a Los Angeles nightclub.

The very features that make camera phones so cool—their small size, portability, and dual function, which allow users to take photos on the sly—also make them a very real workplace danger. Employers have become increasingly worried about employees violating their coworkers' privacy by photographing them surreptitiously at work. Employers that have trade secrets to protect—whether in the form of documents, devices, processes, or personnel—are also understandably afraid that employees might use a camera phone to capture and transmit confidential information.

Camera phones pose a special risk to employers because a user can snap pictures without appearing to do so. And like digital cameras, camera phones allows users to download photos to their computers.

Whether your company's resident photographer is capturing dirty dancing at the company's holiday party or trade secrets on the factory floor ("Let's take a group photo … in front of the dye mixer!"), a camera or camera phone makes it possible for images and information to leave your company in a snap. This chapter explains your policy options for dealing with cameras and camera phones in the workplace. Alternative 1 is an outright ban on cameras and camera phones at work; Alternative 2 allows employees to bring their cameras and camera phones to work, but provides some restrictions on how and where employees may use them.

## Alternative 1: Banning Cameras

The first decision you'll have to make is whether your company should prohibit photographic devices—cameras, video cameras, and camera phones—outright. Note that banning cameras is different from limiting their use, described below in "Alternative 2: Use Restrictions." A ban means employees may not bring cameras to the workplace, period.

### Camera Bans: More Common Than You Might Think

Banning all cameras (and camera phones) in the workplace may seem like an extreme reaction to a somewhat theoretical problem—and, for some companies, that's exactly what it is. But the problems associated with secretly recording others are very real, especially in situations where privacy is at a premium. For example, many fitness clubs, gyms, and swimming pools have banned cameras and camera phones after naked locker room photos began circulating on the Internet. Certain night clubs and other hot spots where celebrities like to mingle ban camera phones. Some hospitals and courthouses also ban camera phones, as do many companies (including camera phone manufacturers, like Samsung and LG).

This is a very restrictive policy choice, suitable only for certain employers. A camera ban may be appropriate if:

- your company works on matters related to national security
- your company has strong confidentiality concerns or valuable trade secrets that can be photographed—for example, machinery, processes, or secret construction, or
- your business provides opportunities for personal privacy violations—for example, employees shower on site after handling hazardous materials.

Because so many cell phones come with a camera feature, an outright ban will pose a real hardship for employees. That's why you'll need to include an exception clause, giving employees who need their personal phones at work a way to get permission to have them.

**No Camera Phones and Other Recording Devices**

The use of cameras, video and audio recording devices, or digital devices, such as cell phones, MP3 players, or PDAs, that have recording capability can cause violations of privacy and breaches of confidentiality.

For that reason, we do not allow cameras, video or audio recording equipment, or cell phones or other digital devices that have these capabilities, on Company property. If you have such a device with you, you may either leave it in your car or [_provide another option, such as "with the receptionist" or "with the office manager"_].

If you believe that your personal circumstances require you to have your cell phone at work, and your cell phone has a camera or other recording capability, please talk to your supervisor.

## Gadgets Without Cameras = Big Corporate Sales Opportunities

After a couple of years when it was almost impossible to find a cell phone without a camera, manufacturers of cell phones and other hand-held devices have started realizing that there's a large potential market for camera-free gadgets. In 2007, for example, Research in Motion released the BlackBerry 8800, a model intended especially for corporate and business use. The 8800 has no camera, at the urging of corporate customers concerned about security. Mike Lazaridis, the company's president, said, "There's a very strong demand out there for BlackBerrys without a camera. Not having one, that's a feature."

Ian Austen, "Can Executives Find Happiness With a Blackberry Without Its Scroll Wheel?," _The New York Times_, February 13, 2007.

# Alternative 2: Use Restrictions

Many companies won't need to ban cameras outright. Instead, you might want to prohibit employees from bringing them into certain areas, prohibit employees from using the camera feature at work, and/or set some guidelines for taking photos at work.

## Prohibiting Cameras in Certain Areas

Most companies can use this policy language, at least for restrooms. Adapt the policy to your workplace by including all areas where cameras could pose a security or privacy risk.

---

**Restrictions on Camera Phones and Other Recording Devices**

Employees may not bring cameras, video and audio recording devices, or digital devices, such as cell phones, MP3 players, or PDAs that have recording capability, to any of the following areas: restrooms, [*other private or secure areas, such as "locker rooms," "changing rooms," "lab," "R & D," "shop floor," and so on*].

---

 **Lessons From the Real World**

**It's a bird! It's a plane! It's a plane photographing our trade secrets!**

In March 1969, employees at DuPont's plant in Beaumont, Texas, noticed a plane circling overhead. DuPont later discovered that the plane held Rolfe and Gary Christopher, who had been hired to photograph new construction at the plant. The Christophers refused to tell DuPont's investigators who had hired them or what they planned to do with the photographs.

DuPont sued the Christophers, claiming they had stolen the company's trade secrets and sold them. DuPont claimed that the photographs depicted an area where DuPont planned to begin producing methanol using a confidential, unpatented process. Because the plant was under construction when the photographs were taken, parts of the process were visible from the air—and DuPont claimed that someone could use this information to piece together its top-secret procedures.

The Christophers argued that they couldn't be sued for trade secret theft because they hadn't violated any laws or any duty to DuPont. They were in public airspace when they took the pictures. Because they didn't work for DuPont, they had no legal obligation to protect its trade secrets. In short, the Christophers argued that they had gotten hold of the photos fair and square, even if they did reveal DuPont's methanol process.

The Court ruled in favor of DuPont, finding that the Christophers had taken its trade secret by "improper means." Had the Christophers or their unnamed client used reverse engineering or independent research to figure out DuPont's process, that would have been fine. But taking it from DuPont without permission, at a time when DuPont was taking precautions to keep the secret, was not.

*E.I. DuPont DeNemours & Co. v. Christopher,* 431 F.2d 1012 (5th Cir. 1970).

## Prohibiting Use of Cameras

Some companies choose to allow employees to bring their camera phones to work, but prohibit use of their recording capabilities. This approach makes sense for many companies, particularly if many employees have camera phones and an outright ban would be met with strong resistance. If your company has privacy and trade secret concerns, you can combine this language with the language above that bans cameras in certain areas, such as restrooms and laboratories.

This type of policy will be difficult to enforce; it can be tough to tell whether someone is actually taking a picture with a camera phone. It will work only if your company has a relatively high level of trust in its employees.

---

**No Use of Camera Phones and Other Recording Devices at Work**

Employees may not use any cameras, video and audio recording devices, or video or recording features of cell phones, MP3 players, PDAs, or other digital devices that contain such capability, at work.

---

### Street Harassment Victims Fight Back—With Camera Phones

First came the camera phone, then the camera-phone voyeur, then the camera-phone crime fighter. You may have heard about "upskirt" photos—or their close relative, "downblouse" photos—taken with camera phones. Typically, these photos are taken surreptitiously. So why have we heard of them? Because there are entire websites devoted to them, where amateur voyeurs can post their photos.

Now, the public harassment tables have turned, with the advent of the antiharassment website. These sites, like Holla Back New York (http://hollabacknyc.blogspot.com), allow readers to post camera phone photos of people who have harassed them in public, along with a narrative of exactly what happened. The blog's motto: If you can't slap 'em, snap 'em.

## Guidelines for Camera Use

Your company may wish to allow employees to use their cameras or camera phones, either in areas where your policy doesn't prohibit such use or only in some situations—for example, at company events or to capture candid photos for a company newsletter. If so, it's a good idea to provide guidelines for taking and using pictures, especially of other employees. This will help you protect employee privacy.

---

**Guidelines for Camera Use**

Employees who use cameras, camera phones, or other digital devices to capture photos or video on Company property or at Company events must follow these rules:

1. Employees may take pictures of other employees, customers, clients, or visitors only with their permission. If you intend to publicize the pictures—for example, by posting them on the Internet, using them in a Company newsletter, or submitting them to a photography contest—you must disclose this to the people whose picture you are taking. If, after taking the pictures, you decide to publicize them in some way, you must obtain permission to do so from the people who appear in them.

2. Employees may not take pictures of Company trade secrets or other confidential information. This includes, but is not limited to, [*list the most common types of trade secrets your company has, such as "customer lists," "pricing information," "recipes," "design plans," "software code," and so on*].

3. Employees may not take or use pictures to harass, embarrass, or annoy others. All Company policies—including the Company's policies on harassment, discrimination, and professional conduct—apply to workplace photographs.

---

4. If you have any questions about whether it's appropriate to take a photograph at work or use a workplace photograph in a particular way, please ask your supervisor.

CAUTION

**Don't forget the acknowledgment form.** If your company adopts the camera phone policy covered in this chapter, make sure you require employees to sign an acknowledgment form. You'll find a sample acknowledgment form and instructions in Appendix B; a blank acknowledgment form is included on the CD-ROM at the back of this book.

## Putting It All Together: Sample Camera Phone Policy

Here's a sample camera phone policy adopted by a (fictional) company that manufactures packaging material. Many employees have cell phones with a camera feature, so the company doesn't want to ban camera phones outright. Also, employees often use their camera phones to take pictures of company parties and employee gatherings for the company's newsletter. But the company is also concerned about employee privacy: Employees change into protective gear at work. And the company wants to keep its manufacturing process confidential. The company decides to prohibit employees from bringing cameras and camera phones into certain areas, and to adopt guidelines for use of cameras at work.

# Camera Phone Policy

### Restrictions on Camera Phones and Other Recording Devices

Employees may not bring cameras, video and audio recording devices, or digital devices, such as cell phones, MP3 players, or PDAs that have recording capability, to any of the following areas: restrooms, locker rooms, the research and development department, and Areas A through D of the plant facility.

### Guidelines for Camera Use

Employees who use cameras, camera phones, or other digital devices to capture photos or video on Company property or at Company events must follow these rules:

1. Employees may take pictures of other employees, customers, clients, or visitors only with their permission. If you intend to publicize the pictures—for example, by posting them on the Internet, using them in a Company newsletter, or submitting them to a photography contest—you must disclose this to the people whose picture you are taking. If, after taking the pictures, you decide to publicize them in some way, you must obtain permission to do so from the people who appear in them.

2. Employees may not take pictures of Company trade secrets or other confidential information. This includes, but is not limited to, the manufacturing line and equipment, specifications for Company products, memos and notes from meetings regarding Company products, all information about products in development, customer lists, and any documents or photographs that have been marked "Confidential: For Internal Use Only."

3. Employees may not take or use pictures to harass, embarrass, or annoy others. All Company policies—including the Company's

policies on harassment, discrimination, and professional conduct—apply to workplace photographs.

4. If you have any questions about whether it's appropriate to take a photograph at work or use a workplace photograph in a particular way, please ask your supervisor.

# How to Use the CD-ROM

The CD-ROM included with this book can be used with Windows computers. It installs files that use software programs that need to be on your computer already. It is not a stand-alone software program.

In accordance with U.S. copyright laws, the CD-ROM and its files are for your personal use only.

Please read this appendix and the "Readme.htm" file included on the CD-ROM for instructions on using the CD-ROM. For a list of forms and their file names, see the end of this appendix.

**Note to Macintosh users:** This CD-ROM and its files should also work on Macintosh computers. Please note, however, that Nolo cannot provide technical support for non-Windows users.

**Note to eBook users:** You can access the CD-ROM files mentioned here from the bookmarked section of the eBook, located on the left-hand side.

---

### How to View the README File

To view the "Readme.htm" file, insert the forms CD-ROM into your computer's CD-ROM drive and follow these instructions:

**Windows 2000, XP, and Vista**
1. On your PC's desktop, double click the **My Computer** icon;
2. double click the icon for the CD-ROM drive into which the forms CD-ROM was inserted;
3. double click the file "Readme.htm".

**Macintosh**
1. On your Mac desktop, double click the icon for the CD-ROM that you inserted;
2. double click the file "Readme.htm".

# Installing the Files Onto Your Computer

To work with the files on the CD-ROM, you first need to install them onto your hard disk. Here's how:

## Windows 2000, XP, and Vista

Follow the CD-ROM's instructions that appear on the screen.

If nothing happens when you insert the CD-ROM, then:

1. Double click the **My Computer** icon.
2. Double click the icon for the CD-ROM drive into which the CD-ROM was inserted.
3. Double click the file "Setup.exe."

## Macintosh

If the **Technology Policy CD** window is not open, double click the **Technology Policy CD** icon. Then:

1. Select the **Technology Policies** folder icon.
2. Drag and drop the folder icon onto your computer.

## Where Are the Files Installed?

### Windows

By default, all the files are installed to the **Technology Policies** folder in the **Program Files** folder of your computer. A folder called **Technology Policies** is added to the **Programs** folder of the **Start** menu.

### Macintosh

All the files are located in the **Technology Policies** folder.

# Using the Word Processing Files to Create Documents

The CD-ROM includes word processing files that you can open, complete, print, and save with your word processing program. All word processing documents come in Rich Text Format and have the extension ".rtf." For example, the Email Policy discussed in Chapter 3 is in the file "Email.rtf." RTF files can be read by most recent word processing programs including MS *Word*, Windows *WordPad*, and *WordPerfect*.

The following are general instructions. Because each word processor uses different commands to open, format, save, and print documents, refer to your word processor's help file for specific instructions.

*Do not call Nolo's technical support if you have questions on how to use your word processor or your computer.*

## Opening a File

You can open word processing files with any of the three following ways:

1. Windows users can open a file by selecting its "shortcut."
    i.  Click the Windows **Start** button.
    ii. Open the **Programs** folder.
    iii. Open the **Technology Policies** folder.
    iv. Open the **RTF** subfolder.
    v.  Click the shortcut to the form you want to work with.
2. Both Windows and Macintosh users can open a file by double clicking it.
    i.  Use **My Computer** or **Windows Explorer** (Windows 2000, XP, or Vista) or the **Finder** (Macintosh) to go to the **Technology Policies** folder.
    ii. Double click the file you want to open.

3. Windows and Macintosh users can open a file from within their word processor.
    i. Open your word processor.
    ii. Go to the **File** menu and choose the **Open** command. This opens a dialog box.
    iii. Select the location and name of the file. (You will navigate to the version of the **Technology Policies** folder that you've installed on your computer.)

## Editing Your Document

Here are tips for working on your document.

- Refer to the book's instructions and sample agreements for help.
- Underlines indicate where to enter information, frequently including bracketed instructions. Delete the underlines and instructions before finishing your document.
- Signature lines should appear on a page with at least some text from the document itself.

### Editing Forms That Have Optional or Alternative Text

Some forms have optional or alternate text:

- With optional text, you choose whether to include or exclude the given text.
- With alternative text, you select one alternative to include and exclude the other alternatives.

When editing these forms, we suggest you do the following:

**Optional text.** Delete optional text you do not want to include and keep that which you do. In either case, delete the italicized instructions. If you choose to delete an optional numbered clause, renumber the subsequent clauses after deleting it.

**Alternative text.** Delete all the alternatives that you do not want to include first. Then delete the italicized instructions.

## Printing Out the Document

Use your word processor's or text editor's **Print** command to print out your document.

## Saving Your Document

Use the **Save As** command to save and rename your document. You will be unable to use the **Save** command because the files are "read-only." If you save the file without renaming it, the underlines that indicate where you need to enter your information will be lost, and you will be unable to create a new document with this file without recopying the original file from the CD-ROM.

| Files on the CD-ROM | | |
|---|---|---|
| **Form Title** | **PDF File Name** | **RTF File Name** |
| Computer and Software Use Policy | Software.pdf | Software.rtf |
| Email Policy | Email.pdf | Email.rtf |
| Internet Policy | Internet.pdf | Internet.rtf |
| Instant Messaging Policy | IM.pdf | IM.rtf |
| Blogs and Personal Posting Policy | Blogs.pdf | Blogs.rtf |
| Cell Phone Policy | Cell.pdf | Cell.rtf |
| Portable Computing Device Policy | PortableComputing Device.pdf | PortableComputing Device.rtf |
| Camera Phone Policy | CameraPhone.pdf | CameraPhone.rtf |
| Electronic Communications and Equipment Policy Acknowledgment Form | Acknowledgment.pdf | Acknowledgment.rtf |

# Acknowledgment Form

In addition to having written technology policies like those covered in this book, every company that monitors—or reserves the right to monitor—its employees' electronic communications and activities must ask employees to sign a form acknowledging that they have read the applicable policies and agree to abide by their terms.

Currently, at least one state (Delaware) requires employers to get written consent before monitoring employees' email or Internet use, and other states consider similar legislation every year.

Even if your state doesn't impose this type of requirement, however, it's a good idea to require a signed acknowledgment. Having to sign a form draws an employee's attention to the policy, which not only makes the employee more likely to comply, but also takes away the employee's ability to argue, later, that he or she had a reasonable expectation of email privacy despite the explicit language of the policy. A signed form also constitutes an employee's consent to employer monitoring, as a legal matter.

Whenever you update your technology policies, you should require employees to sign a new acknowledgment form. (Include the date of the updated policies to avoid confusion.) If your company adopts an entirely new technology policy—perhaps because it decides to issue laptops for the first time or to install GPS tracking in company-owned vehicles—you should require employees to sign an acknowledgment form for that policy as well.

The acknowledgment form below leaves room for you to list the policies to which it applies. Include every policy you have adopted, and every type of equipment you issue to employees.

# Electronic Communications and Equipment Policy Acknowledgment

My signature on this form indicates that I have read the Company's [*list the titles of all technology policies your company has adopted, such as "Computer and Software Policy, Email Policy, Internet Policy, and Cell Phone Policy"*], and I agree to abide by their terms. I understand that any communications I send or receive using Company equipment, including but not limited to email, instant messages, and text messages, are not private, and that the Company may access, monitor, read, and/or copy those messages at any time, for any reason. I also understand that the Company reserves the right to monitor my use of the Internet, and that such monitoring may occur at any time, for any reason.

I understand that all electronic equipment issued to me by the Company, including but not limited to [*list all types of equipment issued to employees, such as "computers, cell phones, laptops, smartphones, and personal digital assistants"*], belong to the Company, and that I must return such equipment upon the Company's request. I also understand that the Company reserves the right to monitor my use of this equipment, and that such monitoring may occur at any time, for any reason.

_____     _____

Employee Signature                                                 Date

_____

Employee Name (Print)

# Index

## A

Accommodation for disabilities, 70
Acknowledgment forms, 19, 187–188
Acronyms, instant messaging, 101
Aerial photographs, 173–174
Anger, in email, 50, 51
Antiharassment websites, 175
Antivirus software, 151, 153, 164
Apple iPhones, 147
Archiving email, 55
Archiving instant messages, 88, 105
Attorney-client privilege, 44
Attorneys, policy advice from, 17, 160
At-will employment, 10
Audio recording devices, 172, 173, 175, 178
Audio streaming, 68, 69, 81

## B

Bandwidth, 11, 40
Basics on technology policies. *See* Technology policy basics
Biometrics, 5, 6
BlackBerry
accessing personal email on, 4
camera-free, 172
for mobile instant messaging (MIM), 85
unpaid overtime and use of, 160
usage statistics, 147
using while driving, 157, 158
Blocked websites, 4, 15, 68–70, 79
Blocking commercial instant messaging software, 89

## Blogs

Blogs
adopting a commonsense policy on, 116–121
"dooced," 119
micro-blogging sties, 110
the positive side of work and, 116
as potentially damaging, 109
prohibiting posts to, 71, 82
restrictions on, 111–116
sample policy on, 122–123
survey on monitoring, 15
use and content statistics, 110
whistlebloggers, 112
Bots, 99
Bouncing messages, 75, 82
Browser history, 4
Buddy list, 85, 99
Business solicitation, employee, 49, 81

## C

Camera bans, 171
Camera-free hand-held devices, 172
Camera phones
banning, 170–172
guidelines for use, 176–179
impact of, 169
pitfalls of, 169–170
policy on, 13, 178–179
street harassment via, 175
use restrictions on, 173–178
Cameras
banning from the workplace, 170–172
guidelines for use, 176–179
real world lesson on, 173–174

# Get the Latest in the Law

### Nolo's Legal Updater
We'll send you an email whenever a new edition of your book is published!
Sign up at **www.nolo.com/legalupdater**.

### Updates at Nolo.com
Check **www.nolo.com/update** to find recent changes in the law that
affect the current edition of your book.

### Nolo Customer Service
To make sure that this edition of the book is the most recent one, call us at
**800-728-3555** and ask one of our friendly customer service representatives
(7:00 am to 6:00 pm PST, weekdays only). Or find out at **www.nolo.com**.

### Complete the Registration & Comment Card ...
... and we'll do the work for you! Just indicate your preferences below:

## Registration & Comment Card

NAME _____ DATE _____

ADDRESS _____

CITY _____ STATE _____ ZIP _____

PHONE _____ EMAIL _____

COMMENTS _____

WAS THIS BOOK EASY TO USE?   (VERY EASY)   5   4   3   2   1   (VERY DIFFICULT)

☐ Yes, you can quote me in future Nolo promotional materials. *Please include phone number above.*

☐ Yes, send me **Nolo's Legal Updater** via email when a new edition of this book is available.

Yes, I want to sign up for the following email newsletters:

  ☐ **NoloBriefs** (monthly)
  ☐ **Nolo's Special Offer** (monthly)
  ☐ **Nolo's BizBriefs** (monthly)
  ☐ **Every Landlord's Quarterly** (four times a year)

☐ Yes, you can give my contact info to carefully selected
partners whose products may be of interest to me.

TECH1

Send to: **Nolo** 950 Parker Street Berkeley, CA 94710-9867, Fax: (800) 645-0895, or include all of
the above information in an email to regcard@nolo.com with the subject line "TECH1."